MW01285281

Busting Through to Greater Freedom:

Dethroning the Counterfeit Trinity

Taking the Bite out of the "ites"

Douglas E. Carr

ISBN:1544122640
ISBN-13:9781544122649

DEDICATION

I dedicate this book to the fine people who make up the congregation of His House Foursquare Church in Sturgis, Michigan. Some of them will have served Jesus alongside me for twenty-five years as of August, 2017. I thank God for them.

It takes a special group of people who will allow their pastor to follow the Lord's call whole-heartedly, even when it includes deliverance ministry, seminars, and much work beyond the local church.

The church stood behind me when I went back to school in 2000, earning my masters and doctorate in deliverance and intercession from Wagner Leadership Institute.

My call to write has been fueled by a congregation which supports me as I preach messages on subjects I'm researching for books. The people understand my calling draws me away from pastoral duties such as regular home visits, attending school functions their children and grandchildren are in, etc.

The call to deep healing and deliverance ministry has made some denominations and former ministry partners look on me with disdain. Thankfully, the small group of people who make up our church has stood with me, supported me, and prayed for me.

Lastly, though most importantly to me, is my wife Pamela. She has always played a big part of my life and ministry in and beyond the local church. She has always heard the Lord for worship and led our worship team into the glory. As my duties outside the local church have expanded, her role within the local church has grown as well. She has taken on the mantle of Pastor for our church. She gives people time and attention I am unable to fit in.

Together, we the people of His House Foursquare Church, are making a Kingdom impact far beyond our city. To each one who supports, prays, worships, gives, helps in many ways – to you I dedicate this book.

ACKNOWLEDGMENTS

Suzanne LeBlanc has again provided valuable help and support, both in editing and computer support to make this book a reality. I thank God for her.

Jeff and Libby Hall came in at just the right time and helped us to believe again and dream again. They used their combined career of fifty years of computer work to help us update our office computer to be compatible with that of my editor and publisher.

Members of the Sturgis Writer's Mill have provided ongoing encouragement and continuing education. They motivate me to keep on writing. Some have carefully read through chapters of the book and given many helpful suggestions.

Arthur Burk of Sapphire Leadership Group, Inc. is a great encouragement to me. He has no idea who I am, but his manifold teachings encourage me to continue seeking and learning.

The International Society of Deliverance Ministers (ISDM) feeds my spirit each year and provides a professional society where I can bounce off new insights in a place of Christian accountability.

Finally, Apostle Barbara Yoder and the Breakthrough Apostolic Ministry Network (BAMN) lead me into greater understanding of what God is up to NOW and Kingdom life as we are to live.

Anything worthy I contribute to the Kingdom is a mixture of what I glean from the people I know from near and afar. I acknowledge them all as contributors to this work.

CONTENTS

FOREWORD
By Suzanne LeBlanc

This book, **Busting Through to Greater Freedom**, unravels the tangled webs of misery, chaos, and disorder weaved about our lives and the lives of those we love and cherish: our families and those among us. Satan's goal is to block us from receiving and being all that the Lord has for us, for the enemy comes to steal what we have, kill whatever he can, and destroy our lives. He does this in the most hidden ways that are simply unfathomable - through the sins (iniquitous patterns and faults or distortions of character that open the doors to sin) of those who have come before us. These are people in generations past that we may or may not even know who have impacted our lives, our children, grandchildren, and the upcoming generations. That seems cruel – even unfair, and it is! How can we guard ourselves against diseases, addictions, emotional and physical abuse, distortions of identity, character impediments, mental/emotional breakdown, etc. that have come down through our bloodline – especially, when we may not even have any knowledge about such things? Satan and his demons target us before we are born, at the time of conception, during fetal development in the womb, and the moment we take our first breath of air and beyond. Once Satan has a foothold, he then spins this web of destruction across generations, within families, societies, and nations. The sins of our forefathers and mothers are passed down across time, which is circular – not linear, and so these sins, reap curses that are repeated over and over again until they are stopped by the breaking of sin via verbal confession and remittance, and applying the blood of Jesus.

In order to stop them, however, we have to first identify the sin committed and/or the patterns of demonic influence that are evident. This may seem impossible. However, nothing is impossible with Christ Jesus! The Lord gives wisdom to the wise and knowledge to those who have understanding, for it is He who reveals the profound and hidden things; He knows what is in the darkness, and the light dwells with Him (Daniel 2:21-22 AMP). Dr. Douglas Carr has mined the Word of God for such revelation – digging deep, excavating the treasures, as revealed by the Holy Spirit, that will break demonic strongholds, tear down demonic structures, and destroy the schemes and blueprint of the enemy from our lives and our bloodlines. Amen!

In this book, Dr. Douglas Carr exposes the wiles of the enemy by examining how the Tribes of Canaan (the Amorites, Jebusites, Hittites, Canaanites, Midianites, Girgashites, Hivites, and Perizzites) impacted the nation of Israel when they entered the promise land, and how these Canaanite Spirits have influenced us through the generations since then to present day. Satan counterfeits whatever God establishes – including God himself. Thus, Dr. Douglas Carr exposes Satan's ploy of a Counterfeit Trinity (Baal, Queen of heaven, and Leviathan) that has wormed its way within nations and how such demonic principalities, powers, and rulers in high places can be dethroned from our midst. Praise God!

On a personal note, I have witnessed the gift of freedom from the Midianite curse. There has always been incredible chaos, strife and contention within my family, and as a result every day has been a battle. Since childhood, every holiday has been wrecked with disappointment, for there has never been any order, harmony, and peace between my parents and siblings. This would escalate every September through April, and this year was certainly no exception. In fact, it was worse. My mom's mental illness suddenly out of control; my dad's arguing over everything was through the roof. I prayed, struggled to maintain peace. In my desperation, I contacted Pastor Doug. He had just finished writing the chapter on the Midianites, so he sent it to me, and I prayed the prayer of release and the Holy Spirit moved powerfully. Within a day, my house was suddenly peaceful, my parents both content, quiet. By the next day, my mom asked me if I had prayed for her. Yes, I had. My mom explained that she was being pulled down a dark path that she could not stop; it was beyond her control. Now, she was joyful, full of peace. Even my adult children who have come to visit have noticed the change, and are simply shocked. For the first time ever, we have enjoyed our family at Thanksgiving and Christmas this past year. What a miracle! What an incredible blessing! I am forever grateful; I thank you Dr. Douglas Carr for the writing of this book.

Yes, it is time to take back our families out the hands of the enemy! Our cities, our nations! Cleanse our bloodlines; prepare the way for the upcoming generations. It's time to receive all that God has ordained for us, be what God has called us to be, and do what we have been called to do, for the Kingdom of God is at hand.

1 CLEANSING BLOODLINES

Cleansing Personal and Cultural Bloodlines: Introduction

The Bible shows we all descended from Adam and Eve. Their generations, however, were reduced to that of Noah and his family after the flood. Noah's naked drunkenness and Ham's indecent behavior toward his father shows iniquity was not wiped out by the flood. The iniquities of personal and cultural ancestors affect us to this day.

North America, especially the United States of America, is a land of foreigners. It's far more difficult for Americans to fill out their family trees than it is for Israelites!

Exodus 20:5 states God visits the iniquity of the fathers to the third and fourth generation. Certain curses, like the curse of illegitimacy are passed down ten generations, and no Ammonite or Moabite or any of their descendants may enter the assembly of the Lord even down to the tenth generation (Deuteronomy 23:2-3). Some good news is, God also shows His love to a thousand generations of those who love Him and keep His commandments (Exodus 20:6).

Thankfully, Jesus shed His blood so we can be redeemed from every curse. IF we apply the blood, we can break personal and ancestral curses and work with others to break curses over our communities and nation. Our purpose in this book is to break the power of iniquities and curses which are passed down bloodlines. We can then release God's purpose and glory over every person, family, city, country, and culture.

Every family & country has a redemptive
purpose established by the Creator.

God's purpose for each person and every people group is redemptive. He created Adam and Eve to steward the earth. He raised up Noah to save a remnant from the flood and give place for our Savior to be born of a woman.

Several Scriptures speak of how God will raise up certain nations for specific times or seasons, including nations used to discipline Israel.

Every family and <u>cult</u>ure has Satanic programming as well.

I underlined "cult" in culture to illustrate how Satan tries to corrupt cultures and countries. All have sinned and fallen short of the glory of God, and Satan wants to use common cultural human iniquity to hinder entire people groups from advancing the glory of God's Kingdom on earth.

There's controversy over who the first humans were in North America.

a. Were they Vikings?

Some believe the first Europeans here were Vikings led by Leif Ericson in 1000 AD. An article in Wikipedia says

> The Vikings came from Norway, Sweden, Iceland and Denmark (Scandinavia in Northern Europe). They called American "Vinland," and the Viking Settlement they found could be one of many.[1]

b. Were they from Southeast Asia and the Southern Pacific area?

An interesting article in *National Geographic News* shares the debate over the colonization of the Americas. Some believe Native Americans descended from northeast Asia over a land bridge between Siberia and Alaska some 12,000 years ago. Stefan Lovgren suggests:

> "Our results change the traditional idea that all modern Amerindians present morphological affinities with East Asians as a result of a single migration," said Rolando González-José of the University of Barcelona, Spain, who led the study. "The settlement of the New World is better explained by considering a continuous influx of people from Asia."[2]

c. Were they "Indians" (Native Americans)?

"Native American" is more respectful than "Indian" when referring to those often considered to be the First People to inhabit this land. Most believe the name "Indian" was a misnomer by Christopher Columbus. Yahoo Answers provides insight on this:

> The term Indians as applied to Native Americans, or the indigenous peoples of the Americas, is thought to have originated in a misconception on the part of the Europeans who arrived in Central America in 1492. Since Christopher Columbus began his journey to America with the intent of finding an alternate route to Southeast Asia, he is said to have assumed that the people he came into contact with upon reaching land were Indians. Despite the fact that people probably realized this mistake within hours, the name remained in use. Similarly, the islands in Central America came to be called the "West Indies," as opposed to the "East Indies" that Columbus originally had in mind as his destination.[3]

d. One thing for sure is whomever the first people were - they were sinners.

Since all have sinned and fallen short of the glory of God, we know the first inhabitants of North America were sinners (Romans 3:23). The wages of sin is death (Romans 6:23a) and Satan uses personal and ancestral sin to kill, steal, and destroy (John 10:10a.). Thankfully, the free gift of God is eternal life through Christ Jesus (Romans 2:23b) and Jesus came that we might have life more abundantly (John 10:10b). So how do we move from personal and corporate death and destruction to the redemptive purposes of God? We began by addressing personal, ancestral, and cultural iniquity.

e. Barry Fell gives evidence of Baal's influence on America.

In 1975 an archeological survey of New Hampshire and Vermont revealed "hundreds of inscriptions among the ruins attest the vitality of Celtic civilization in pagan times, and tell a wonderful story of how Europeans lived in the Bronze Age."[4]

On page 54 of the same book Fell tells how they discovered the name of the sun god Bel on the lintels of temples dedicated to sun worship in Vermont. His book is a fascinating study which challenges our thinking of whom the first people of America are.

The First Step of Breaking Generational Iniquitous patterns is Confessing and Renouncing Personal Iniquities and Faults.

Many Bibles substitute the word "sins" for iniquities. Iniquity is deeper than sin which is missing the mark. It means a bent, distortion, or twisting of character. As we confess and repent of ungodly character bents and receive prayer from those who have overcome such bents we can be healed of them. Deliverance is not complete unless we deal with iniquity. I wrote about this in *Getting to the Dirty Rotten Inner Core*:

> God began revealing keys to inner core issues as I looked at the greater meaning behind the Hebrew and Greek words best translated "iniquities" and "faults." He showed me that deliverance deals with demons and deep healing deals with inner wounds and that is needed. But neither of these fully addresses the inner core of iniquities and faults.[5]

James 5:16 encourages us to confess our personal faults to each other. Faults – not just a sin here or there, but the bent or distortion of character that leads to sin. As we confess those faults (bents, twisting, and distortion of character) to each other we can receive prayer from the righteous (those who do not share a particular iniquity or who have overcome it) and be healed of that iniquity! I share how to do this in *Getting to the Dirty Rotten Inner Core*.

The Second Step of Breaking Personal or Cultural Iniquitous Patterns is Confessing and Renouncing Ancestral iniquities and Faults.

I have preached at the Coldwater Jail, near my home, once a month since 1988. It is amazing how many inmates are in jail for iniquities they inherited from their ancestors. More amazing is how people carry ancestral bents and distortions of absentee parents and grandparents they never knew! Sin is passed down through the blood.

a. Ancestral iniquities and problems are passed down generationally.

The Bible books of Kings and Chronicles often speak of doing evil or committing sins as the fathers have done. Here are some examples:

📖 He did evil in the sight of the Lord, as his fathers had done; <u>he did not depart from the sins of Jeroboam</u> the son of Nebat, which he made Israel sin. 2 Kings 15:9 NASB. ^(Underlined for emphasis)

📖 And they that are left of you shall pine away in their iniquity in your enemies' lands; and <u>also in the iniquities of their fathers shall they pine away with them.</u> Leviticus 26:39 KJV. ^(Underlined for emphasis)

The word translated "pine away" means to lose vigor, health, or flesh, as through grief. The King James Dictionary defines "pine away:"

> 1. To languish; to lose flesh or wear away under any distress of anxiety of mind; to grow lean; followed sometimes by away. 2. To languish with desire; to waste away with longing for something; usually followed by for.[6]

Such ancestral iniquity can be devastating if not confessed, repented of, and covered with the blood of Jesus.

📖 <u>Both their own iniquities and the iniquities of their fathers together,</u>" says the Lord. "Because they have burned incense on the mountains and scorned Me on the hills, Therefore I will measure their former work into their bosom." Isaiah 65:7 New American Standard Bible. ^(Underlined for emphasis)

📖 Our fathers sinned, and are no more; <u>It is we who have borne their iniquities.</u> Lamentations 5:7 NASB. ^(Underlined for emphasis)

God added a warning to the Second Commandment showing how iniquity is passed down especially when idolatry is practiced. That will be important to remember as we continue our study.

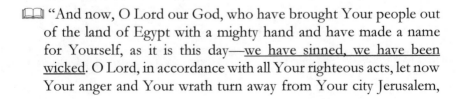 You shall not worship them or serve them; for I, the Lord your God, am a jealous God, <u>visiting the iniquity of the fathers on the children, on the third and the fourth generations</u> of those who hate Me. Exodus 20:5 NASB. ^(Underlined for emphasis)

b. Iniquity is passed down all branches of the family tree.

I used to think iniquity was only passed down through fathers, grandfathers, and the male gender because it says "iniquity of the fathers." Many wives and mothers probably think that too! After over twenty years of deliverance ministry, however, I couldn't help but notice how the iniquities of mothers and grandmothers are also passed down. I asked the Lord about this and He simply said "Don't you think I meant that 'one flesh' thing."

c. Iniquity may be passed down through adoption, step-parents, and god- parents as well.

I can only give experiential verification of this as I have not yet found scriptural proof. It seems to me demons take advantage of any type of legal guardianship to pass down curses, iniquities, demons, dedications, and judgments.

It may not warrant much space here, but God ordained each office, including government, church, business, family, etc. to be holy unto Him. When people within those offices sin, they pollute the office and demons may take up residence in the office. So, if the office of a father or mother has been polluted, children coming under that authority may inherit iniquitous patterns and curses spawned from them.

d. Scriptural examples of confessing the iniquities of the Fathers:

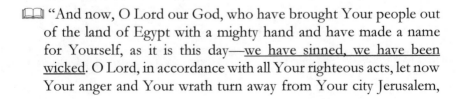 The descendants of Israel separated themselves from all foreigners, and stood and <u>confessed their sins and the iniquities of their fathers</u>. Nehemiah 9:2 NASB. ^(Underlined for emphasis)

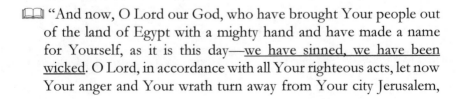 "And now, O Lord our God, who have brought Your people out of the land of Egypt with a mighty hand and have made a name for Yourself, as it is this day—<u>we have sinned, we have been wicked</u>. O Lord, in accordance with all Your righteous acts, let now Your anger and Your wrath turn away from Your city Jerusalem,

Your holy mountain; for <u>because of our sins and the iniquities of our fathers</u>, Jerusalem and Your people have become a reproach to all those around us. <u>So now, our God, listen to the prayer of Your servant</u> and to his supplications, and for Your sake, O Lord, let Your face shine on Your desolate sanctuary. Daniel 9:15-17 NASB. (Underlined for emphasis)

The Third Step of Breaking Generational Iniquitous Patterns is Confessing and Renouncing Political Iniquities and Faults.

a. Iniquities, sins, and corresponding judgments, strongholds, demons, and bondage can be passed through leaders to followers.

When church leadership falls into sexual sin it opens the doors for sexual sin among the members until leadership confesses and renounces the sins of the leaders. Those doors remain open until they are closed – even years or decades after a leader has left. I've seen that in churches I've pastored and others I have ministered in.

President Bill Clinton opened gateways for the enemy to bring new level of perversion to our children when he had oral sex with Monica Lewinski. The Obama administration opened gateways to perverse marriage and relationships which fall under Baal's control. May heaven close the gates opened to perversion through "legalizing" same sex marriage and flying rainbow flags in our country, Israel, and over businesses.

b. Scriptural examples of confessing cultural iniquities:

Daniel taught us we need to confess personal, ancestral, and political iniquity.

📖 [8]<u>Open shame belongs to us</u>, O Lord, <u>to our kings, our princes and our fathers, because we have sinned against You</u>. [11] Indeed <u>all Israel has transgressed Your law and turned aside</u>, not obeying Your voice; so the curse has been poured out on us, along with the oath which is written in the law of Moses the servant of God, for we have sinned against Him. [12]Thus He has confirmed His words which He had spoken against us and <u>against our rulers who ruled us</u>, to bring on us great calamity. Daniel 9:8, 11, 12a NASB. (Underlined for emphasis)

We need to pray! Corruption has increased from generation to generation. We MUST pray.

c. Terrorists find open portals through national iniquity.

Is national iniquity a greater threat than ISIS? I believe it is! Ezra clearly states how society was given over to be plundered because of personal and national guilt! Israel's God is always more powerful than heathen gods and nations, but when people transgress His laws, He hands them over to be plundered.

📖 Since the days of our fathers to this day we have been in great guilt, and on account of our iniquities we, our kings and our priests have been given into the hand of the kings of the lands, to the sword, to <u>captivity and to plunder and to open shame</u>, as it is this day. Ezra 9:7 NASB. (Underlined for emphasis)

There is battle for the throne of each region.

I stumbled across some notes which I believe are from a Regional Leader's meeting with Barbara Yoder. She encouraged us to believe the Scriptures and begin strategizing how we might advance the Kingdom of God in our region. I wish I would have taken better notes, but I share a couple of Scriptures she referenced and a few notes I took.

a. Jesus has the mandate to establish His throne of justice and righteousness.

📖 For to us a child is born, to us a son is given, and <u>the government will be on his shoulders</u>. And he will be called Wonderful Counselor, Mighty God, Everlasting Father, Prince of Peace. [7]<u>Of the greatness of his government and peace there will be no end</u>. He will reign on David's throne and over his kingdom, establishing and upholding it with justice and righteousness from that time on and forever. The zeal of the Lord Almighty will accomplish this. Isaiah 9:6-7 NIV. (Underlined for emphasis)

b. Jesus delegated His authority to His Church to advance His Kingdom.

📖 ¹⁸And I tell you that you are Peter, and on this rock I will build my church, and the gates of Hades will not overcome it. ¹⁹<u>I will give you the keys of the kingdom of heaven; whatever you bind on earth will be bound in heaven, and whatever you loose on earth will be loosed in heaven.</u>" Matthew 16:18-19. ^(Underlined for emphasis)

📖 Then said Jesus to them again, Peace be unto you: as my Father hath sent me, even so send I you. John 20:21 KJV.

c. Individuals will be judged according to how they occupy till Jesus returns.

📖 And he called his ten servants, and delivered them ten pounds, and said unto them, occupy till I come. Luke 19:13 KJV.

A parable is an earthly story with a heavenly meaning. In the parable of the talents Jesus tells of ten servants who were each given a mina (around $225.00) and told to use it to be about the business of the king until he returned. He then focused on three of those servants and blessed the two who increased the mina five or ten times, and gave them authority over five and ten cities. He then judged the one who hid and did not increase the mina given to him – he took that mina and gave it to the man who had ten.

The Greek word translated "occupy" in the King James Version is only used in this passage. *Barnes notes* say:

Occupy till I come - The word "occupy" here means not merely to "possess," as it often does in our language, but to "improve," to employ "in business," for the purpose of increasing it or of making "profit" on it. The direction was to use this money so as to gain "more" against his return. So, Jesus commands his disciples to "improve" their talents; to make the most of them; to increase their capability of doing good, and to do it "until" he comes to call us hence, by death, to meet him.[7]

An article I read from *His Sheep* adds:

Back to our mandate. What is that mandate? Simply put in Luke 19:13, "Occupy till I come." It means to be busy, to be occupied doing something, to do business till I come, to work hard till I come and to give His kingdom and His gospel full attention until He comes.[8]

Apostle Barbara Yoder says "Occupy" means we need to knock the devil out. We need to take the seat/throne of authority. I think she is closest to what Paul wrote:

📖 His intent was that now, <u>through the church</u>, the manifold wisdom of God should be made known <u>to the rulers and authorities in the heavenly realms</u>, [11]according to his eternal purpose that he accomplished in Christ Jesus our Lord. Ephesians 3:10-11. (Underlined for emphasis)

We are to be Jesus' personal assistant to demolish strongholds and regain God's redemptive purposes for individuals, families, cities, states, and nations.

I once had a Frank and Ernest cartoon in my office. One mentioned, "I've been thinking about asking God why He doesn't do something about all the crime and poverty in our world." The other said "Why don't you?" And the first answered, "I'm afraid He might ask me the same question."

We are Christ's ambassadors on earth. We are to re-present Him, His mission, righteousness, and judgment on this earth. I ran across some notes I took, perhaps at our ISDM meeting, but I failed to record who said it. They listed God's personal assistants.

God's Personal Assistants:
Gabriel   is Holy Spirit's personal assistant.
Michael   is Jehovah's personal assistant.
Lucifer   was Jesus' personal assistant.
Church   NOW is Jesus' personal assistant.[9]

Jesus says His Kingdom IS advancing and forceful kingdom people lay hold of it. In the same context, He says he who is least in the Kingdom of heaven is greater than John the Baptist.

Kingdom people -- Let's occupy till He comes!

I encourage the reader to pray the following prayer over what we have covered thus far and move on to an introduction to the Canaanite Spirits. It is important to vocalize such prayers, because unlike God, Satan cannot hear our silent prayers, and spoken prayers will break his hold. As Luther wrote in *A Mighty Fortress is our God:* "one little word will fell him."

Prayer:

- Father God, Jesus calls us to be a victorious church which overcomes the world and advances the Kingdom of God on earth.
- We confess we and our ancestors have failed to complete that mission.
- Jesus, You gave us the keys to the Kingdom. We confess we and our ancestors have failed to use these keys as we ought.
- You told us we can bind and loose things on earth as in heaven.
- We need Your help in doing so.
- You anointed us with power and authority and commissioned us to make disciples of all nations (see Matthew 28:18-20).
- Help us to put our hands to the plow and do that without turning back.
- You told us forceful people lay hold of the Kingdom of God (Mt. 11:12).
- Today we ask Your help in laying hold of the Kingdom.
- Jesus, you told us to seek FIRST Your Kingdom and Your Righteousness (Mt. 6:33).
- We are here today to do just that! Help us to lay hold of Your Kingdom.
- In Jesus' Name and through His blood. Amen.

Introduction to Canaanite Spirits.

We must be aware we are engaged in spiritual warfare whether we want to be or not. Paul tells us we have a host of spiritual enemies.

📖 Finally, my brethren, be strong in the Lord and in the power of His might. Put on the whole armor of God, that you may be able to stand against the wiles of the devil. For we do not wrestle against flesh and blood, but against principalities, against powers, against the rulers of the darkness of this age, against spiritual hosts of wickedness in the heavenly places. Ephesians 6:10-12 NKJV.

We are at war against the same powers and principalities that hindered Israel from walking in total victory. The Canaanite Spirits work against Believers to kill, steal and destroy. They worked through ungodly tribes to resist the Israelites as they moved from Egypt and pressed to enter the fullness of their destiny as they moved into the Promise Land. They continue their work now to hinder us from fulfilling our destinies.

I first did this study while working on my Masters using Harold Dewberry's teachings as a foundation. A few years ago, I read The Seven Mountain Prophecy by Johnny Enlow. He connects the Canaanite tribes with the seven mountains that God wants us to rule for the Kingdom! He gives a full chapter to each of the tribes and has a chart that summarizes them in the back.

THE EXAMPLES OF THE BATTLE:

a. Paul's Example:

📖 For I do not want you to be ignorant of the fact, brothers, that our forefathers were all under the cloud and that they all passed through the sea. They were all baptized into Moses in the cloud and in the sea. They all ate the same spiritual food and drank the same spiritual drink; for they drank from the spiritual rock that accompanied them, and that rock was Christ. Nevertheless, God was not pleased with most of them; their bodies were scattered over the desert. Now these things occurred as examples to keep us from setting our hearts on evil things as they did. Do not be idolaters, as some of them were; as it is written; "The people sat down to eat and drink and got up to indulge in pagan revelry." We should not commit sexual immorality, as some of them did--and in one day twenty-three thousand of them died. We should not test the Lord, as some of them did--and were killed by snakes. And do not grumble, as some of them did--and were killed by the destroying angel. These things happened to them as examples and were written down as warnings for us, on whom the fulfillment of the ages has come. So, if you think you are standing firm, be careful that you don't fall! No temptation has seized you except what is common to man. And God is faithful; he will not let you be tempted beyond what you can bear. But when you are tempted, he will also provide a way out so that you can stand up under it. 1 Corinthians 10:1-13 NIV. ^(Underlined for emphasis)

b.   The APPLICATION of the Examples:

Then the LORD (Jehovah) said to Moses, "Now you will see what I will do to <u>Pharaoh</u>: Because of my mighty hand he will let them go; because of my mighty hand he will drive them out of his country." God also said to Moses. "I am the LORD. I appeared to Abraham, to Isaac and to Jacob as God Almighty, but my name the LORD I did not make myself known to them. I also established my covenant with them <u>to give them the land of Canaan</u>, where they lived as aliens. Moreover, I have heard the groaning of the Israelites, whom the Egyptians are enslaving, and I have remembered my covenant. Therefore, say to the Israelites: `I am the LORD, and I will bring you out from under the yoke of the Egyptians. <u>I will free you from being slaves to them</u>, and I will redeem you with an outstretched arm and with mighty acts of judgment. I will take you as my own people, and I will be your God. Then you will know that I am the LORD your God, who brought you out from under the yoke of the Egyptians, and I will bring you to the land I swore with uplifted hand to give to Abraham, to Isaac and to Jacob. I will give it to you as a possession. I am the LORD.'" Moses reported this to the Israelites, <u>but they did not listen to him because of their discouragement and cruel bondage</u>." Exodus 6:1-9 NIV. ^(Underlined for emphasis)

This is the beginning of the story of how the Israelites could have escaped from bondage. They got a good start, but unfortunately, most of them did not make it all the way into the Promise Land. Their story leaves an example that encourages us not to give up until we are totally free from bondage and every stronghold of the enemy is torn down. Why do you think it is important to study the tribes which tormented Israel? Each one of them represents a spiritual enemy that wars against Believers.

c. The PATTERN of the Examples:
1. Pharaoh is a pattern of the DEVIL.
2. Egypt is a pattern of the WORLD.
3. Israelites are a pattern of the called-out ones - CHRISTIANS.
4. The Journey is a pattern of our daily BATTLE.
5. The Promised Land is a pattern of HEAVEN.
6. The Rock is a pattern of CHRIST.
7. Going through the sea is a pattern of our BAPTISM.
8. Their lives are a pattern of the SPIRITUAL WARFARE we face.

**Whichever side they chose to identify with
and walk with became the side that won.**

I first studied the Canaanite tribes and spirits while working on my Masters using Harold Dewberry's teachings as a foundation. A few years ago, I read The Seven Mountain Prophecy by Johnny Enlow.[10] He connects the Canaanite tribes with the seven mountains that God wants us to rule for the Kingdom! He gives a full chapter to each of the tribes and has a chart that summarizes them in the back. We will go over them in the order they confronted the Israelites as they entered the Promised Land. Let's pray before continuing our journey:

The Canaanite Tribes & Corresponding Spirits:
- Father, we confess and repent of every place we and our personal and cultural ancestors have cooperated with Canaanite spirits.
- In Jesus' Name and through His blood, we bind the Canaanite Strongman and demolish his stronghold. We bind the demons working under command.
- Father bring us revelatory truth concerning each tribe we study.
- Help us to respond to this truth that will set us free.

Endnotes:

[1]http://en.wikipedia.org/wiki/VinlandPer

[2]Who Were The First Americans? Stefan Lovgren for National Geographic News September 3, 2003.

[3]https://search.yahoo.com/search?p=Why+were+native+americans+called+%22Indians%22&fr=ush-mailn_02&fr2=p%3Aml%2Cm%3Asb

[4]*America B.C.*, Barry Fell, Demeter Press Book. Sixth printing 1977. Page 5.

[5]*Getting to the Dirty Rotten Inner Core*. Douglas Carr, Create Space 2014.

[6] http://av1611.com/kjbp/kjv-dictionary/pine.html

[7]*Barnes' Notes* on Luke 19:13. http://www.godvine.com/

[8] http://occupytillicome.ca/images/image3.gif

[9]Possibly from the 2015 annual meeting of the International Society of Deliverance Ministers.

[10]*The Seven Mountain Prophecy: Unveiling the Coming Elijah Revolution Paperback* –Johnny Enlow, Creation House 2008.

2 AMORITE INTRODUCTION

When I first began studying curses, I wrote 29 days of devotions on how the curse against Canaan followed his family for generations causing all sorts of problems in the family line. I realized how a careless curse, like the one spoken by a hero like Noah against Canaan, can bring devastation to one generation after another in his family line. Genesis records how the curse took root.

📖 When Noah woke up with his hangover, <u>he learned what his youngest son had done. He said, Cursed be Canaan</u>! A slave of slaves, a slave to his brothers! Blessed be God, the God of Shem, but Canaan shall be his slave. God prosper Japheth, living spaciously in the tents of Shem. But Canaan shall be his slave. Genesis 9:24-27 MSG. ^(Underlined for emphasis)

Amorite is first mentioned in a genealogy of Canaan.

📖 Canaan begot Sidon his firstborn, and Heth; [16]the Jebusite, the <u>Amorite</u> . . . Genesis 10:15a-16 NKJV. ^(Underlined for emphasis)

God warned Israel of Canaanite tribes before they entered the Promised Land.

📖 When the Lord your God brings you into the land which you go to possess, and has cast out many nations before you, <u>the Hittites and the Girgashites and the Amorites and the Canaanites and the Perizzites and the Hivites and the Jebusites, seven nations greater and mightier than you,</u> [2]and when the Lord your God delivers them over to you, you shall conquer them and utterly destroy them. <u>You shall make no covenant with them nor show mercy to them.</u> [3]Nor shall you make marriages with them. You shall not give your daughter to their son, nor take their daughter for your son. Deuteronomy 7:1-3 NKJV. ^(Underlined for emphasis)

"Amorite" means "mountain people; renowned." Since mountains refer to tall majestic land masses that dominate over valleys, we see how the Amorite spirit is a spirit of self-exaltation. The Hebrew word for Amorite comes from another word, "amar" which means, "to utter, to say."" People with Amorite spirits want their names in the limelight. Amorites are fame-seekers. They want to be glorified in their greatness, like Lucifer. Most dictators are Amorites: Adolph Hitler, Joseph Stalin, Fidel Castro, Saddam Hussein, and North Korean leader Kim Jong Un who loves to flaunt his missiles are possessed by Amorite spirits. They want to dominate and control others, have their pictures plastered all over, and demand their subjects submit to their dominion and perhaps even revere and worship them.

The Amorite spirit is alive and well working through many politicians, and educators who have exchanged the truth of God for a lie. Johnny Enlow, author of *The Seven Mountain Prophecy*, teaches the Amorite spirit represents humanism and is over the mountain of education, working under the principality Beelzebub who is the father of lies.[1]

Have you ever wondered about the bewitching power of humanistic education to turn our children away from Biblical faith? The Jewish Encyclopedia says, Amorites are "Masters of Witchcraft— In Rabbinical and Apocryphal Literature."[2]

Just as mountains dominate over landscape, Amorites want to dominate and rule over others. They tend to establish an imposing and seemingly immovable presence. The Amorite curse gives way to Amorite spirits.

Amorite spirits, empowered by the curse, continue surprise attacks.

📖 Though the Israelites warred against the Amorites and defeated them on occasion, they continued coming back like birthday candles that relight themselves. Do you ever ponder why wicked people seem to get away with their sin for long periods of time? In Genesis fifteen God gave a span of four generations for the Amorites to either repent or be given over to full moral depravity. In the fourth generation your descendants will come back here, <u>for</u>

the sin of the Amorites has not yet reached its full measure."
Genesis 15:16 NIV. (Underlined for emphasis)

Amorite spirits lead to pride and boasting.

As mountain people, the Amorites looked down on others.

📖 The Amalekites dwell in the land of the South; the Hittites, the
Jebusites, and the Amorites dwell in the mountains; and the
Canaanites dwell by the sea and along the banks of the Jordan."
Numbers 13:29 NKJV. (Underlined for emphasis)

Amorite refusal to cooperate impedes progress.

Whether in church, minister's, or business meetings, there are
always some who boastfully stand against what others want to do.
Amorite spirits are often behind such behavior.

📖 Then Israel sent messengers to Sihon king of the Amorites, saying,
"Let me pass through your land. We will not turn aside into fields
or vineyards; we will not drink water from wells. We will go by the
King's Highway until we have passed through your territory." But
Sihon would not allow Israel to pass through his territory. So Sihon
gathered all his people together and went out against Israel in the
wilderness, and he came to Jahaz and fought against Israel.
Numbers 21:21-23 NKJV. (Underlined for emphasis)

The battle against Amorite isn't over until it's over!

Israel ended up defeating the Amorites after Sihon came out
against Israel, but they still had to fight that group time and again. They
took possession of many cities, but many battles continued to be won
or lost.

Personal or group rebellion make way
for Amorite spirits to attack.

📖 "Nevertheless you would not go up, but rebelled against the
command of the Lord your God; and you complained in your
tents, and said, 'Because the Lord hates us, He has brought us out
of the land of Egypt to deliver us into the hand of the Amorites,
to destroy us.' Deuteronomy 1:26-27 NKJV. (Underlined for emphasis)

Bill Sudduth, leader of ISDM, said "there are two ways to get rid of demons—you can starve them out or cast them out."[3] One reason rebellion is the sin of witchcraft is whenever people rebel against the authority God has placed over them, it opens them to satanic attack. That is what is seen here: Israel's disobedience gave opening for the Amorites to kill, steal, and destroy.

Amorite stirs up discouragement through negative reports.

📖 Where can we go up? <u>Our brethren have discouraged our hearts</u>, saying, "The people are greater and taller than we; the cities are great and fortified up to heaven; moreover we have seen the sons of the Anakim there." Deuteronomy 1:28 NKJV. (Underlined for emphasis)

Moses sent out twelve spies. Can you think of any of their names? You may remember the name of the two who were men of faith and great leaders (Joshua and Caleb). Ten were fearful and faithless. Guess who the people listened to? Not the two men of faith and vision, but the ten who brought negative reports. Satan will do anything he can to stir up a few people among a body of believers to convince others godly vision cannot be fulfilled and that God is not able.

Amorite uses bee-like fear to throw people off course.

I remember when my five-year old son bumped a paper hornets' nest. He started screaming and running and I was paralyzed by fear for a moment until my love for him threw me into action to run after him and protect him from the attack. Amorite spirits use fear of what might happen to drive people out of their prophetic destinies.

📖 The Amorites who lived in that hill country came out against you and <u>chased you as bees do</u>, and crushed you from Seir to Hormah. Deuteronomy 1:44 NASB. (Underlined for emphasis)

Amorite lures you to retreat.

Many denominations push one retreat after another. My wife Pamela says it is time to advance, not retreat! We can't let the enemy convince us to retreat or take our hands off the plow. The greatest resistance comes just before breakthrough. This calls for advance, not retreat! (No, I am not against God ordained Sabbath rest, vacations and like.)

When individuals or groups keep taking three steps forward and two steps back, it may be an Amorite at work.
This even affected the great leader Joshua.

📖 Joshua said, "Alas, O Lord God, why did You ever bring this people over the Jordan, only <u>to deliver us into the hand of the Amorites, to destroy us? If only</u> we had been willing to dwell beyond the Jordan! Joshua 7:7 NASB. ^(Underlined for emphasis)

Remarks like "If only, "would've, could've, should've" never accomplish anything. Paul urges us to forget what is behind and press forward to the prize.

Amorite uses speech to open demonic gateways.

📖 <u>Death and life are in the power of the tongue,</u> And those who love it will eat its fruit. Proverbs 18:21 NKJV. ^(Underlined for emphasis)

I love Peterson's paraphrase in *The Message* of Psalm 5:9:

📖 Every word they speak is a land mine; their lungs breathe out poison gas. Their throats are gaping graves, their tongues slick as mudslides. Pile on the guilt, God! Let their so-called wisdom wreck them. Kick them out! They've had their chance. Psalm 5:9 MSG.

Amorite perverts speech so what we say will crush people.

📖 A wholesome tongue is a tree of life, but perverseness in it crushes the spirit. Proverbs 15:4 MEV. ^(Underlined for emphasis)

II. THE ORIGIN of SPEECH:

📖 Speech has the power to bless, liberate, and set us free. It also has power to take us captive and make us vulnerable to evil spirits. Think of how God created words to create! In the beginning was the Word, and the Word was with God, and the Word was God. [2]He was with God in the beginning. John 1:1-2 NIV.

Jesus is the very beginning of the spoken word. Jesus was active in creation's "Let us."

📖 And God said, Let there be light: and there was light .... And God said. Let there be a firmament in the midst of the waters, and let it divide the waters from the waters. And God said, Let the waters under the heaven be gathered together unto one place, and let the dry [land] appear: and it was so .... And God said, Let there be lights in the firmament of the heaven to divide the day from the night; and let them be for signs, and for seasons, and for days, and years .... And God said, Let the waters bring forth abundantly the moving creature that hath life, and fowl [that] may fly above the earth in the open firmament of heaven .... And God said, Let the earth bring forth the living creature after his kind, cattle, and creeping thing, and beast of the earth after his kind: and it was so .... And God said, Let us make man in our image, after our likeness: and let them have dominion over the fish of the sea, and over the fowl of the air, and over the cattle, and over all the earth, and over every creeping thing that creepeth upon the earth .... And God said, Behold, I have given you every herb bearing seed, which [is] upon the face of all the earth, and every tree, in the which [is] the fruit of a tree yielding seed; to you it shall be for meat. From Genesis 1:3, 6, 9, 14, 20, 24, 26, 29. KJV (Underlined for emphasis)

Creation came into existence by the speaking of God's Word. When God spoke it, it happened. There are two words that mean the same in Greek and Hebrew. The Greek "rhema" and the Hebrew "Dabar" both mean "the word," but they also mean "the thing." They can be used interchangeably because in God's eye the spoken word can become the thing, depending on the context of use.

📖 As it is written: "I have made you a father of many nations." He is our father in the sight of God, in whom he believed—the God who gives life to the dead and calls things that are not as though they were. Romans 4:17 NIV. (Underlined for emphasis)

When God speaks something, He considers it done. When He said light, there was light. As far as God is concerned, when it is spoken, it is. This concept carries on throughout Scripture where Rhema or Dabar is used. God is the creator of the word. God creates by speaking and demonstrates it in creation itself.

III. Examples of the Power of Speech:

The Tower of Babel.

God confused the language to keep them from building a "tower to heaven." John Maxwell said God was afraid of what man was going to do in Genesis 11:6. Look:

📖 The LORD said, "<u>If as one people speaking the same language</u> they have begun to do this, then <u>nothing they plan to do will be impossible for them</u>. Come, let us go down and confuse their language so they will not understand each other." Genesis 11:6-7 NIV. ^(Underlined for emphasis)

Nothing can stop people from doing what they want as long as they speak the same language.

In Genesis Chapter Eleven, God confused the languages so people bent on false worship would not be able to. Then in Acts two, when Holy Spirit was poured out upon the church everyone heard the message in his own language! It was in this power of such unified understanding of speech the greatest revival ever was poured out.

Nothing is impossible when we speak the same language, for there is power in what people say with their mouths-especially when said in a context of unity.

The power of united prayer.

When the early Christians raised one voice in prayer they were given power for healings, signs, and wonders.

📖 Now, Lord, consider their threats and enable your servants to <u>speak your word</u> with great boldness. Stretch out your hand to heal and perform miraculous signs and wonders through the name of your holy servant Jesus." <u>After they prayed, the place where they were meeting was shaken</u>. And they were all filled with the Holy

Spirit and spoke the word of God boldly. Acts 4:29-31. NIV.
(Underlined for emphasis)

We will get the same results when we join in prayer!

The power of voices lifted in one accord.

In Acts 12, James was arrested and put to death by sword. That pleased the Jews so much Herod arrested Peter. James' death propelled the church to a higher level of prayer and intercession.

📖 Peter therefore was kept in the prison; <u>but unceasing prayer was made</u> by the assembly to God concerning him. Acts 12:5 DBY.
(Underlined for emphasis)

Their prayers saved Peter from execution! An angel came and led him out of prison. It's ironic, the church was praying fervently for Peter, but when he showed up at Rhoda's doorstep, where they were praying for his release, they accused Rhoda of being out of her mind for saying Peter was at the door. They even said "it must be his angel" (See Acts 12:13-16). This proves the power of words! Even though they didn't believe God had answered their prayers, He had!

The power of words to invoke the
glory of God's manifest presence.

In 2 Chronicles 6:21-7:2, Solomon dedicated the temple and asked God to arise in their midst. Fire came down from heaven and the glory of the Lord filled the temple. The priests couldn't even enter the temple because God's glory was so thick. I look back at Sundays when God manifests powerfully in our services. There are times I'm barely able to minister because He is so close. The only thing I know we have done differently on such occasions is we have intentionally invoked His presence and lingered before Him. They waited and only moved when the cloud moved.

The power of agreeing in prayer.

Jesus spoke of the power of agreement.

📖 "Again I say to you, that <u>if two of you agree</u> on earth about anything that they may ask, <u>it shall be done</u> for them by My Father who is in heaven. Matthew 18:19 NASB. (Underlined for emphasis)

According to this, IF we break into groups of two or three and pray for the glory of the Lord to be revealed, it will happen. It will be done even as we say it. All we need is a few people speaking a thing out together. The problem we have is too many mixed voices. The glory of God doesn't fall because God only moves by that which he speaks or by that which is spoken by us in unity, and too few Christians are speaking together in unity.

IV. Good Things Come from Speaking in Unity:

Deliverance, healing, prosperity, and blessing come as we agree with the Word of God and with other godly people by what we speak with our mouths. As we muscle out the word of God unceasingly, that which is spoken in our hearts through meditation comes to pass in our lives.

Deliverance.

David knew the words of his mouth, spoken in prayer, would bring deliverance from the evil men who surrounded him. He would speak the words in prayer, and God would give relief.

📖 When I call, give me answers. God, take my side! Once, in a tight place, you gave me room; Now I'm in trouble again: grace me! hear me! Psalm 4:1 MSG.

Forgiveness, cleansing, and remitting.

Do you think anyone can truly repent without speaking? Repentance includes confessing, which is verbalizing agreement with God, through spoken prayer, that we agree with His judgment concerning our sin. David knew the power of repentance when the words were spoken out. As David agreed with God about his own sinful condition by speaking out in confession, His sins were forgiven and he was purified.

Psalm 51:1-10 gives a beautiful picture of how David spoke words of confession and repentance after being convicted concerning his sin with Bathsheba and Uriah the Hittite. There is a human component to that story, however, we often overlook. We remember how Nathan the Prophet rebuked David for his sin, but we may forget how Nathan responded to David's confession by saying "your sin is forgiven." David still paid some of the consequence of his sin, in that his son died, but Nathan's words relieved David's guilt to where he could pray what he wrote in Psalm 51.

📖 Then David said to Nathan, "I have sinned against the Lord." Nathan replied, "<u>The Lord has taken away your sin</u>. You are not going to die. 2 Samuel 12:13 NIV. ^(Underlined for emphasis)

I wish every translation of John 20:23 would give the richness and power of the word "remit" like Darby and a few other translations do. Oxford Dictionaries on line give this definition of remit:

Verb: cancel or refrain from exacting or inflicting (a debt or punishment):
Noun. the task or area of activity officially assigned to an individual or organization.[3]

Consider the task given you by Jesus as you consider His words, rightly translated by Darby:

📖 And having said this, he breathed into [them], and says to them, Receive [the] Holy Spirit: <u>whose soever sins ye remit, they are remitted to them</u>; whose soever [sins] ye retain, they are retained. John 20:22-23 DBY. ^(Underlined for emphasis)

Nathan remitted David's sin which lead him to his prayer in Psalm 51. As to underscore the emphasis of this point, Holy Spirit led me to respond to a buzz on my phone. It was an email from a minister who came for deliverance two days earlier. We didn't make it nearly as far as I had hoped with his questionnaire, but we dealt with a lot on forgiving as well as confession upon which I repeatedly said "Your sin is remitted – as far as the east is from the west, so far has the Lord removed it from you." He wrote:

I would like to thank you for taking your valuable time with me on Monday, to bring me into a greater freedom than I've ever experienced in my walk with Christ, of 27 + years. In the short time that has passed I've noticed several significant visible changes.

I've not raised my voice and can't handle loudness of those speaking to me. My purpose in prayer and my ministering the Word last night in our feeding center. I seemed to flow even closer to the Father's heart for His children to return to Him, with a repentant heart of change and desire for Him. I've had some revelations on how to conduct ministry business to ease the financial strain that we have felt in the past years. This was the case this morning, when my wife and I were beginning morning prayers.

While I am continuing to look into and be aware of The Holy Spirit's voice to reveal things I need to repent of and release to Him for removal from my mind soul and spirit.

I just want to be closer to Him, than I can even imagine being. (He died in an accident 2 weeks later.) He is my reality and His closeness to me will I am completely sure will bring me greater life flowing through my spirit to other's. Especially my family.

Blessings to you both and your very vital ministries to the body of Christ.

This man had not sinned greatly since his salvation, but the power of his testimony came through the power of spoken words remitting confessed sins! We've witnessed many who have cheated on their spouses, or had abortions, or fallen into pornography set free when we have simply used the power of words to remit sins and cast out demons.

The power of the voice of triumph.

When I was first introduced to church as a boy, I was taught to be silent in church, especially after I became an altar boy. Such silence, however, has more to do with religion than with biblical expressions of worship. As the Psalmist said,

📖 Clap your hands, all you nations; shout to God with cries of joy. Psalm 47:1 NIV.

The context of Psalm 47 shows we need to use our voice as a shout of triumph against the enemy! When Israel did so, God entered their battle and gave them victory. When Israel went against Jericho they went on a word fast for six days as they marched around the city of Jericho. I believe this was so they would quit sharing negative words for demons to enter.

Whining never brings victory!

Think what would have happened to their faith and confidence had people started murmuring and complaining: "We've never done it this way before," "Who does Joshua think He is?" "The Lord speaks to me too, and I haven't heard him tell me to walk around the walls like a bunch of dumb sheep."

God wisely had them fast speaking for six days. Then on the seventh day they marched around the city and when Joshua had the trumpets sounded the people shouted in one accord and the walls came tumbling down at their voice of triumph. (Joshua 5:13-6:27)

The power of the sword of the Spirit

Paul says the word of the Spirit is the rhema word of God (words spoken under Holy Spirit inspiration).

📖 Take .... the sword of the Spirit, which is the word of God. Ephesians 6:17 NIV.

A very special word is used for "the word of God" here and in Romans 10:17. It is the word "rhema" which refers to words spoken through utterance of the Holy Spirit. As humans speak the words given by Holy Spirit, they happen! As we speak God's word against the enemy it wounds him. Between writing this and preaching it, a woman from Detroit called. I have not met her but have had a few phone and email conversations with her. She was in terrible pain, and assumed it was from the curses of her Satanist neighbors. I simply prayed as Holy Spirit gave utterance. She began weeping. Her pain went from a ten to zero! The power of positive words given by Holy Spirit.

The power of fruitful words.

All words bear fruit, but words spoken from the fruit of the Spirit in one's life have the power to bring positive change in one's own life and the lives of others. A positive Spirit led "way to go," builds up while a negative condemning "way to go" tears people down.

📖 From the fruit of his lips a man is filled with good things as surely as the work of his hands rewards him. Proverbs 12:14.

God releases great change as people learn to speak the fruit of the Spirit into their lives: love, joy, peace, patience, kindness, goodness, faithfulness gentleness, and self-control. I think of the man who was shopping with a fussy and screaming child. The father seemed to be doing ok. He kept saying "Take it easy, Albert, everything is going to be ok." "Watch your temper, we'll be going home soon." A lady shopper bent over the cart, caressed the child and said "What's wrong Albert?" And the father said "Oh, no - that is Billy - I'm Albert"

The power of words in healing.
📖 Pleasant words are a honeycomb, sweet to the soul and healing to the bones. Proverbs 16:24.

There is power in proclaiming good health over yourself. I've seen people become sick at the mention of looking sick. "You don't look very good, are you feeling all right?" I've also seen people start to feel better when they were told they look better. I am not talking about lying to ourselves or speaking as a condition is not there. Instead I suggest we speak God's truth to ourselves: such as "and the prayer offered in faith will make the sick person well" and "Through his stripes we are healed."

We need to go a little deeper in our study on the Amorite curse and spirit as we continue our study, but for now, let's receive, by faith, what we have covered thus far.

You will often notice the word (Expel!) following certain prayers throughout this book. James tells us to "resist the devil and he will flee" (James 4:7). The best way I've learned to resist the devil in prayer is to blow, cough, or yawn by faith. I've found it interesting how children usually yawn when going through deliverance. Even more interesting is how adults who were demonized as children yawn as they resist demons that attached to them in childhood.

Prayers of release from the Amorite Curse/Spirit:
⟩ Heavenly Father, in the Name and through the blood of Jesus, I confess where I and my ancestors have spoken boastfully, exalted

ourselves over others, or have sought vainglory through position or title.

❧ I confess where I and my forefathers have used the power of words to manipulate or control others.

❧ I repent of cooperating with the Amorite spirit.

❧ Father, I ask you, in Jesus' Name and through his blood, to break every Amorite curse brought upon me and my family line by iniquity and sinful behavior, especially regarding speech.

❧ I am redeemed by the blood of the Passover Lamb from the hand of the enemy.

❧ Father, I ask You to bind and rebuke Baal and the strongmen of Canaanite and Amorite.

❧ With the divine weapons you have given, we demolish the strongholds of Baal, Canaanite, and Amorite.

❧ I come against Amorite spirits and cast them out in Jesus' Name. (Expel)

❧ I ask Abba Father to cast out the strongmen of Baal, Canaanite, and Amorite. (Expel)

❧ I cast out Beelzebub and lying spirits. (Expel)

Now let's pray the prayer of Psalm 141:3-4 NKJV:

❧ Set a guard, O Lord, over my mouth;

❧ Keep watch over the door of my lips.

❧ Do not incline my heart to any evil thing,

❧ To practice wicked works

❧ With men who work iniquity;

❧ And do not let me eat of their delicacies.

❧ In Jesus' name, Amen.

Endnotes:

[1]The Seven Mountain Prophecy – Johnny Enlow – Summary Sheet. http://www.the7mountains.com/2010/01/24/the-seven-mountain-prophecy-johnny-enlow-summary-sheet/
[2]1906, Jewish Encyclopedia, by: W. Max Muller, Kaufmann Kohler http://jewishencyclopedia.com/
[3]Bill Sudduth, President, Righteous Acts Ministries, Inc. Apostolic leader, International Society of Deliverance Ministers.
[4]Powered by OxfordDictionaries @ Oxford University Press.

3 AMORITE POWER OF WORDS

Beelzebub is called "Lord of the Flies." Flies represent his lies. They represent humanism, atheism, liberalism and rationalism. The word Amorite means to speak, to speak against, to boast about, act proudly. Such speech always opens gateways to the devil's activity.

We have two daughters, one has a daycare and the other is a kindergarten teacher. They both witness the power words have on children to build them up or tear them down. As a boy, I often heard words like "You don't have the brains God gave a goose," "you're not worth a Tinker's damn," and "you're not worth the teats on a bore hog." Is it any wonder I was a problem student through my high school graduation? Thankfully I came to know Abba Father who speaks encouragement and life, so I did well in college and graduate studies.

Ministers of deep healing spend hours with people who struggle to enter their prophetic destiny because of the power of words to oppress, shame, and destroy. Praise God, people can be led to forgive those whose words hurt them. They can renounce hurtful words and break agreement with them. They can come into agreement with what God says over them.

The power of negative words is seen time and again in life and in Scripture. Most people remember only two of the names of the spies sent to spy out the Promised Land. (Caleb and Joshua in whom there was a different spirit). The names of the other ten, whose negative words led Israel into forty wasted years wandering in the desert, are forgotten and their graves are probably never visited. Their negative words led to the death of most of their generation before they ever entered the promises of the lord.

The negative words of the spies of Israel. (Numbers 13:1-16)
The Children of Israel were held in bondage by negative words of the spies. They gave a bad report which led the people to doubt and

rebellion. This was the Amorite spirit at work. I looked up the meanings of the names of these twelve spies.

➤ Shammua means "Rumor." (Remember the game "rumor?" Rumor is not a game!)
➤ Shaphat means "Judged."
➤ Caleb means "dog or slave." (He rose far above his name!)
➤ Igal means "He redeems." (His negative words hindered God's goal for their lives.)
➤ Joshua (Hoshea) means "salvation."
➤ Palti means "Delivered." (Unfortunately, they were delivered into the hands of Satan, not from them.)
➤ Gaddiel means "Fortune of God." (Gaddiel and Gaddi are a picture of the prosperity God wanted them to have . . .)
➤ Gaddi may mean "Fortune or Fortunate."
➤ Ammiel means "My kinsmen is God." (They sure didn't act like family!)
➤ Sethur means "Hidden."
➤ Nahbi means "Concealed or hidden." (Secrecy is not a value of the Kingdom!)
➤ Geuel means "Majesty of God." (Their negativity made them miss His majesty.)

Surprisingly, seven of the twelve names were positive, two of them could be positive or negative, depending on one's sense of adventure, and only three of them were negative. Isn't that the way negative words work? The Amorite spirit uses negative words to bring people of great promise down.

Even a few negative words open paths of bondage and defeat.
Someone who studies speech said:

In 1990 there was an average of 4 criticisms to every affirmation. In 2000, the average was 11 criticisms to every affirmation. Amorite is at work! (Source unknown)

The doubting words of Zechariah.
Zechariah and Elizabeth prayed for a child their entire married life. They prayed past the age of childbearing and had given up hope. Zechariah was a faithful priest and actually doing annual priestly duties in the Holy of Holies when an angel came and shared the good news

they would have a son. Think of this: Zechariah was busy doing very special ministry when he was visited by the angel, yet his response was one of doubt.

📖 And Zacharias said to the angel, How shall I know this, for <u>I am an old man</u>, and <u>my wife advanced in years</u>? And the angel answering, said to him, I am Gabriel, who stand before God, and I have been sent to speak to thee, and to bring these glad tidings to thee; and behold, <u>thou shalt be silent and not able to speak</u>, till the day in which these things shall take place, because thou hast not believed my words, the which shall be fulfilled in their time. Luke 1:18-20 DBY. (Underlined for emphasis)

God loved Zechariah enough to keep negative words from warring against the promise of God, so He put him on a forced word fast. Knowing the power of negative words, God rendered him speechless! Suzanne LeBlanc suggested this word fast may have also broken the power of negative words from Zechariah's bloodline so John the Baptist would not receive the same speech patter his father had! The name John means "gracious." How could John have proclaim the truth of Jesus and the Kingdom if this was not broken off his bloodline? Zechariah went for nine months without being able to speak any negative, doubtful, self-condemning, or hopeless words. After this word fast of doubting words, he was a changed man!

📖 Then they made signs to his father, to find out what he would like to name the child. He asked for a writing tablet, and to everyone's astonishment he wrote, "His name is John." <u>Immediately his mouth was opened and his tongue was loosed, and he began to speak, praising God</u>. His father Zechariah was filled with the Holy Spirit and prophesied: "Praise be to the Lord, the God of Israel, because he has come and has redeemed his people." Luke 1:62-68 NIV. (Underlined for emphasis)

This is the first record of Zechariah prophesying with power! It took a nine-month word fast to disconnect him from negative words and to release words of faith. After fasting from negative speech, he was able to speak under the anointing of Holy Spirit with words of freedom and deliverance.

His words which were pathetic became prophetic!

Consider Jesus' warning about negative words:

📖 "You have heard that it was said to the people long ago, 'Do not murder, and anyone who murders will be subject to judgment. 'But I tell you that anyone who is angry with his brother will be subject to judgment. Again, <u>anyone who says to his brother,</u> 'Raca', is answerable to the Sanhedrin. But anyone who says. 'You fool!' will be in danger of the fire of hell. "Therefore, if you are offering your gift at the altar and there remember that your brother has something against you, leave your gift there in front of the altar. First go and be reconciled to your brother; then come and offer your gift. Matthew 5:21 -24 NIV. ^(Underlined for emphasis)

Jesus warned of the danger of speaking evil, slanderous words. Raca means "empty, vain, worthless." Think of Jesus' words the next time someone cuts you off while driving, or the next time a family member ticks you off.

Don't call someone worthless, vain, empty headed, because if you do you will be in danger of the council. The word fool means "rebel, outlaw, reprobate." Calling someone a reprobate or rebel will subject us to judgment!

Moses boastful words prevented his entrance to the Promise Land.

"Amorite" means "to speak, to speak against, to speak boastfully." Have you ever wondered why God fired Moses from his assignment to take the Israelites into the Promise Land? All he did was strike the rock, just like God told him to the first time they needed water. The water did gush out just like it did before, but God wasn't happy. This time God had told Moses to speak to the rock but Moses "did it like he always had done it." Does it seem extreme to you that Moses was sentenced to die in the wilderness because he struck the rock rather than speak to it? Look for yourself.

📖 The LORD said to Moses, "Take the staff, and you and when your brother Aaron gather the assembly together. <u>Speak to that rock</u> before their eyes and it will pour out its water. You will bring water out of the rock for the community so they and their livestock can drink." So Moses took the staff from the LORD'S presence, just as he commanded him. He and Aaron gathered the assembly together in front of the rock and Moses said to them, "<u>Listen, you rebels, must we bring you water out of this rock</u>?" Then Moses raised his arm and struck the rock twice with his staff. Water gushed out, and the community and their livestock drank. But the LORD said to Moses and Aaron, "Because you did not trust in me enough to honor me as holy in the sight of the Israelites, you will not bring this community into the land I give them." These were the waters of Meribah, where the Israelites quarreled with the LORD and where he showed himself holy among them. Numbers 20:7-13 NIV. (Underlined for emphasis)

Moses struck the rock when God told him to speak to it.

Paul tells us that rock was Christ (1 Corinthians 10:4)! Moses had to strike the rock the first time because it pictured Jesus who had to be smitten. When Moses struck the rock a second time it pictured him re-crucifying Christ in the sight of the congregation. That was so serious in God's eyes that Moses wasn't allowed to lead the people into the Promise Land.

When people react rather than respond to situations, Amorite may be at work.

God gave me a new phrase while I was preaching at the jail. He said: "I will change your reactions into RESPONSE-ability." Under Holy Spirit inspiration I shared how God wants to transform us to where, rather than reacting, we will respond according to the Holy Spirit's leading in every situation!

Amorite wants people to react according the flesh. God wants us to respond in the Holy Spirit. Reaction brings death and destruction. Response by the Holy Spirit brings life and edification.

Moses reacted rather than responding to the complaints of the people. "Listen, you rebels, must we bring you water out of this rock?" Moses fell into pride and anger because of the complaining of the people. He blew it – acting as if he could, in his own power, produce the water. Moses learned the hard way about the danger leaders face when people to provoke their spirits and they say things with their mouths they shouldn't be saying. Paul gives warning of that for when we help backsliders:

📖 Brothers, if someone is caught in a sin, you who are spiritual should restore him gently. <u>But watch yourself, or you also may be tempted</u>. Galatians 6:1-2 NIV. (Underlined for emphasis)

The congregation's complaining words.

Moses was out of order as the leader, but the people are responsible as well. They drove Moses to a point of frustration so he lashed out rash words that led the entire nation to defeat and walking in circles in the wilderness of sin. Psalm 106 shows this caused everyone problems.

📖 By the waters of Meribah they angered the LORD, <u>and trouble came to Moses because of them</u>: for they rebelled against the Spirit of God, and rash words came from Moses' lips. Psalm 106:32-33 NIV. (Underlined for emphasis)

The critical, self-promoting words of Miriam and Aaron.

Leaders carry great responsibility and God judges them according to how they steward that responsibility. At the same time, however, God pays very close attention when people begin speaking evil of their leaders.

📖 <u>Miriam and Aaron began to talk against Moses</u> because of his Cushite (Ethiopian) wife, for he had married a Cushite. "Has the LORD spoken only through Moses?" they asked. "Hasn't he also spoken through us?" <u>And the LORD heard this</u>. (Now Moses was a very humble man, more humble than anyone else on the face of the earth.) At once the LORD said to Moses, Aaron and Miriam, "Come out to the Tent of Meeting, all three of you." So the three of them came out. Then the LORD came down in a pillar of cloud; he stood at the entrance to the Tent and summoned Aaron and Miriam. When both of them stepped forward, he said, "Listen to my words: "When a prophet of the LORD is among you, I reveal myself to him in visions, I speak to him in dreams. But this is not true of my servant Moses; he is faithful in all my house. With him I speak face to face, clearly and not in riddles; he sees the form of the LORD. <u>Why then were you not afraid to speak against my servant Moses?</u>" The anger of the LORD burned against them, and he left them. When the cloud lifted from above the Tent, there stood Miriam-leprous, like snow. Aaron turned toward her and saw that she had leprosy; and he said to Moses, "<u>Please, my lord, do not hold against us the sin we have so foolishly committed</u>. Do not let her be like a stillborn infant coming from its mother's womb with its flesh half eaten away." So Moses cried out to the LORD, "O God, please heal her!" The LORD replied to Moses, "If her father had spit in her face, would she not have been in disgrace for seven days? Confine her outside the camp for seven days; after that she can be brought back." So Miriam was confined outside the camp for seven days, and the people did not move on till she was brought back. Numbers 12:1-15 NIV. ^(Underlined for emphasis)

Miriam and Aaron illustrate what murmuring does. There is nothing wrong with speaking out truth in love. God had spoken through Miriam and Aaron too. What they said about Moses divorcing his first wife, a Midianite and marrying a second wife, the Ethiopian woman was true. But they spoke the truth slanderously. Moses was divorced and had married an Ethiopian woman. Ethiopian means a new beginning of a new family and that upset Miriam and Aaron. They murmured against Moses with their mouth. They had a right to speak the truth - but only in love. The way they spoke showed envy and jealousy. They spoke the truth but not in humility and love, and were therefore brought before judgment. Look at how quickly judgment came. Verse two says "And the Lord heard it!"

God moved suddenly! Notice, Moses didn't try to defend himself, but God defended him. Miriam became leprous because of the way she spoke the truth about leadership. What happened to her was bad enough. When someone tries to promote themselves by criticizing leadership, it not only hurts the person, it hinders the entire congregation. Everyone was delayed in their forward progress because of her negative words.

Many families, churches, and ministries have been held back because the Amorite spirits works in leaders and followers to mutter bad reports. My reputation as a man of prayer proved itself in 2001 when the city asked me to lead first responders in prayer and then put together a prayer event after the terrorist attacks on the Pentagon and World Trade Towers. It felt like we were close to revival when the town came together to pray.

A few years later, however, unfounded rumors and bad reports allowed Amorite room to attack when I vigorously opposed a casino coming to Sturgis. Letters were written to the editor saying I was out of touch with the needs of our area, and didn't care if people couldn't find jobs if the casino wasn't allowed to be built just south of town. Thank God, Sturgis does not have a casino! There is still need, however, for the people of God to break the hold of the Amorite spirits over our lives and ministry.

Miriam had leprosy when the cloud lifted. Aaron cried out a prayer everyone should pray if they have allowed Amorite to control their tongue.

**"Please, my lord, do not hold against us
the sin we have so foolishly committed!"**

The sad results of Miriam's wrong talking:

The Lord departed.

He wasn't with them anymore. He walked away and left them to themselves and their sin.

The Glory Cloud departed.

The glory of the Lord was no longer in their midst. They came to church, but God wasn't there. Pam and I were enjoying lunch one Sunday when people at a table nearby began tearing their pastor apart. I knew I never wanted to visit their church – God probably didn't want to either!

Miriam was stricken with leprosy.

Many illnesses would be healed if people would only speak healthy words, but the power of life and death are in the tongue.

Progress came to a standstill.

The glory of the Lord departed and the congregation could not move forward because they murmured against leadership.

Is that why church altars are empty? Is that why the church isn't moving forward and God's church in Sturgis isn't growing? Has the Amorite spirit won the battle for our families, church, and community?

HOW TO CHANGE YOUR WORDS INTO BLESSING:

Recognize the power of words over our spirits.

I hear so many people making negative comments about themselves, their health, their spouses, jobs, etc. They can't seem to find God in any of their circumstances. Satan loves to take advantage of little phrases people speak: "I'm so stupid, I will never get it right, I give up."

What would happen if we spoke Ephesians 3:20 over ourselves and one another? There is no greater power at work within than the power of the Word. Jesus is the Word and His entire existence demonstrates how the power of words brings things into being.

📖 Now to him who is able to do immeasurably more than all we ask or imagine, according to his power that is at work within us, to him be glory in the church and in Christ Jesus throughout all generations, for ever and ever! Amen. Ephesians 3:20 NIV.

We must tell our human spirits to rule our souls.

📖 Like a city whose walls are broken down is a man who lacks self-control. Proverbs 25:28.

Part of discipleship must include working out our salvation with fear and trembling. We must rule our human spirits and tell them to control out thoughts, emotions, and wills. We need to tell our human spirits to reign and rule over soul and body. We need to consciously come into right spiritual alignment and bring our souls and bodies into subjection to our human spirits. If we do that, Amorite spirits and curses will be rendered powerless.

📖 For those who <u>live according to the flesh set their minds on the things of the flesh</u>, but <u>those who live according to the Spirit, the things of the Spirit</u>. For to be carnally minded is death, but <u>to be spiritually minded is life and peace</u>. Romans 8:5-6 NKJV. ^(Underlined for emphasis)

We must control our tongues for good and not evil.

We can build ourselves and others with our tongues, or we can destroy with the tongue. Many are weak in body because they are weak in spirit. They are weak in spirit because of the of perverseness of tongue and corresponding breach in the spirit.

We must utilize the power of proclamation.

Jesus proclaimed:

📖 "The Spirit of the Lord is upon Me, Because He has anointed Me <u>To preach</u> the gospel to the poor; He has sent Me to heal the brokenhearted, <u>To proclaim</u> liberty to the captives And recovery of sight to the blind, To set at liberty those who are oppressed; <u>To proclaim</u> the acceptable year of the Lord." Luke 4:18-19 NKJV. (Underlined for emphasis)

How do we loose captives and set them free? By proclamation. Proclaim the day of liberty, proclaim the gospel, proclaim the acceptable year of the Lord's favor. Proclaim revival is coming to the Gateway city. Proclaim great healings and deliverance.

We choose sides through the power of words. James wrote:

📖 You adulterous people, don't you know that friendship with the world is hatred toward God? Anyone who chooses to be a friend of the world becomes an enemy of God. Or do you think Scripture says without reason that the spirit he caused to live in us envies intensely? But he gives us more grace. That is why Scripture says: "God opposes the proud but gives grace to the humble." Submit yourselves, then, to God. Resist the devil, and he will flee from you. Come near to God and he will come near to you. Wash your hands, you sinners, and purify your hearts, you double-minded Grieve, mourn and wail. Change your laughter to mourning and your joy to gloom. Humble yourselves before the Lord, and he will lift you up. Brothers, do not slander one another. Anyone who speaks against his brother or judges him speaks against the law and judges it. When you judge the law, you are not keeping it, but sitting in judgment on it. There is only one Lawgiver and Judge, the one who is able to save and destroy. But you—who are you to judge your neighbor? James 4:4-12 NIV. (Underlined and bold print for emphasis)

We humble ourselves as we choose to speak God's way! God releases His grace when we speak as He tells us to speak. God says submit, and if we agree we are yielded to Christ. God tells us to resist the devil and if we agree the devil will flee.

God *won't* do it without our agreement and we *can't* do it without Him.

God told me something recently that changed my stance in spiritual warfare. I had fallen into the trap of focusing first on the devil and what he is up to before focusing on and submitting to God and what He is doing and saying.

May His words bless you as they do me: *You experience far more attack than attachment, but you resist first by coming to me and then going against the devil. Submit first; resist second. This will become a by word for you.*

Regardless of what battles we are in, God wants us to focus first on Him so we will receive strategy to win life's battles.

We must cling to His spoken promises.

His divine power has given us everything we need for life and godliness through our knowledge of him who called us by his own glory and goodness. Through these he has given us his very great and precious promises, so that through them you may participate in the divine nature and escape the corruption in the world caused by evil desires. 2 Peter 1:3-4 AMP. (Underlined and bold print for emphasis)

God has given us the keys of the Kingdom. We can forcefully advance the Kingdom in our lives, families, church, city and country if we will stand guard over our lips.

We can control everything by controlling our tongues.

We all stumble in many ways. If anyone is never at fault in what he says, he is a perfect man, able to keep his whole body in check. James 3:2 NIV. (Underlined for emphasis)

Emotional maturity is shown through controlling of the tongue. If we don't control the Amorite spirit's work of negative or boastful speech, it will control us!

We must recognize the power of speaking in agreement.

📖 "Again, I tell you that if <u>two of you on earth agree</u> about anything you <u>ask for,</u> it will be done for you by my Father in heaven. For where two or three come together in my name, there am I with them." Matthew 18:19-20 NIV. ^(Underlined for emphasis)

Johnny Enlow says the Amorites (represent humanism) and work in the mountain of education under the principality Beelzebub (lies).[1]

I say the Amorite spirit works through the power of the tongue. We have a sword which is the Word of God! We have the truth which is our shield and buckler! It is time to quit believing the devil's lies and begin speaking God's truth. We need to put away all negative speech, and speak only that which is good for edifying others in the Lord! If people will not quit speaking negative, complaining and whining words they will never be delivered. If, however, we conquer the Amorite curse and spirit we will be able to stand against the wiles of the devil and we will win. Let's join together with or words and declare the battle. Let us break Amorite curses and cast down Amorite spirits.

Ministry to break Amorite curses and spirits:

- ҂ Father we confess and repent of all personal and ancestral boasting, complaining, and hurtful speaking.
- ҂ We confess and repent of all personal and ancestral believing or speaking lies, falsehood, or slander.
- ҂ We confess and repent of all personal and ancestral reacting according to the flesh rather than responding by the spirit.
- ҂ We confess and repent of all personal and ancestral of where we have given in to Amorite curses and spirits.
- ҂ In the Name and through the blood of Jesus, we break every Amorite curse off ourselves, our families, our church, city, and nation.
- ҂ We cast down: all lying spirits, every Amorite spirit, and Beelzebub.
- ҂ In the mighty name of Jesus who is the way, the truth and the life. (Expel)
- ҂ We ask You, Father, to break the power of Amorite and humanism off our schools.
- ҂ Please bring our children and grandchildren into Your truth which will set them free.
- ҂ We pray the God of peace will sanctify us through and through and that our spirits will rule over our souls, bodies, and especially our tongues.
- ҂ In Jesus' name. Amen.

Endnotes:

[1]The Seven Mountain Prophecy – Johnny Enlow – Summary Sheet. http://www.the7mountains.com/2010/01/24/the-seven-mountain-prophecy-johnny-enlow-summary-sheet/

4 JEBUSITE

Johnny Enlow summarizes the work of Jebusite thus: Jebusite spirits are assigned to the Mountain of Family and represent rejection. They work under the principality Baal (perversion) to displace the significant authority of Pastors who have the basic mission to impact social systems so that the family unit is prioritized. Revelation 5:12 Key: Strength.[1]

Based on ministering deliverance since 1995 and deep healing since 2000, I believe Jebusite may be one of the most destructive of all curses and demonic assignments, as it tramples people through dysfunctional family relationships. Unfortunately, many pastors are trained to counsel but don't understand how curses and demons work to undermine people in the very areas they seek counsel.

Jebusite works under Baal to bring rejection to family and the biblical mandate for family being a husband, wife, and children.

Jebusite means "treading or trodden down to defeat, pollute and defile." It is on mission to destroy family as God ordained it. It represents condemnation, pollution and defilement. This spirit makes one feel guilty or condemned. It traps people by grief over weaknesses and failures and brings them under condemnation. In Isaiah 14:19 it says "Who go down to the stones of the pit, like a corpse trodden underfoot." Arguing, abuse, separation, and divorce tear children and adults apart and makes them feel walked on.

The word "Jebusite" comes from the Hebrew word for "under foot."

This spirit builds strongholds in carnal appetites and desires. Such desires open portals for ruling spirits to usurp control over one's life.

America is weak because her churches are weak, churches are weak because her families are weak. Families are weak because husbands and wives are weak. God calls pastors to shepherd families and impact social systems so family is prioritized. This will release God's strength in the earth realm. Government, schooling, and churches cannot bring transformation apart from the family unit.

Jebusite works to displace parents as primary care-givers for children. Schooling is essential for children, but God's design is for parents to oversee a child's education. School activities must never replace family. When children or parents are too busy to spend time together, they are busier than God wants them to be! Parents must maintain the role as primary nurturer of children. They should never surrender their calling as parents to anyone else, including the public-school system or church! In Galatians, Paul makes it clear that fathers are responsible to oversee their children, not educators or other guardians.

📖 Now I say that the heir, as long as he is a child, does not differ at all from a slave, though he is master of all, but is under guardians and stewards <u>until the time appointed by the father.</u> Galatians 4:1-2 NKJV. (Underlined for emphasis)

Parents discipline their children so they will learn self-discipline and self-control. Far too many adults and children are ruled by their flesh rather than by the Spirit of God working in and through their human spirits. The Bible still tells parents to apply the "board of education to a child's seat of understanding." Judge for yourselves whether children are better off since corporal punishment has been removed from homes and schools. Parents must believe and heed what Proverbs has to say about disciplining children. God still knows what is best!

Teens tend to be legalists, stretching the law to the furthest extent so they can get away with as much as possible. Parents are mandated to first teach little children what to do, and later teach them why.

I love the way Peterson paraphrases this concept in The Message:

📖 Just because something is technically legal doesn't mean that it's spiritually appropriate. If I went around doing whatever I thought I could get by with, <u>I'd be a slave to my whims.</u> 1 Corinthians 6:12 MSG. (Underlined for emphasis)

Jebusite is on mission to destroy children, marriages and families. The day before writing this I received a tearful call from a precious wife and mother of four young precious children. She gave me five-minute warning her husband was backing out of the very appointment that could save his life and their marriage. I soon learned what I feared was true. He was letting Jebusite destroy his home and marriage through another woman. Thankfully God intervened, but the children already have felt the brunt of what Jebusite wanted to do to their family.

Jebusite takes advantage of every opening to sow rejection.

When Jebusite sows into one spouse, the other spouse often begins to reject the one they perceive is rejecting them. Both build walls around their hearts to protect from them further pain. Like Earthquakes and aftershocks, blow ups or separation in a family cause seismic waves of rejection in all directions. When one leaves a spouse, the rejection is very real and leaves incalculable damage. When there are children, they absorb the rejection and take it personally. Psychologically, children, especially oldest sons, tend to blame themselves for their parent's divorce and absorb it as personal rejection. Rejection begets rejection, which begets more rejection. A person with a strong "rejection complex" will send out strong vibes that say "please reject me," inviting ongoing rejection. That is one reason blended families struggle to survive emotionally, when all family members carry strong rejection baggage. Parents of such families need to face any damage which has been done and address it with prayer and counsel.

Rejection by a father, whether real or perceived, comes with another severe price tag: it often warps the developing sexual identity of little boys or girls. A boy will tend to seek male approval endlessly, becoming confused and often crossing a sexual line into abnormality. In young girls, the flower of being a woman never opens, and a father's rejection tempts them to never again desire anything from a man. When Jebusite demons do this level of emotional damage, they have prepared their prey for the principality atop this mountain.

Jebusite means "thresher" and refers to walking on people.

"Jebusite" means "thresher," and refers to beating grain out of the husk. This was usually done through oxen who were used to tread on the grain laid out over a "threshing-floor." From this we can infer Jebusite, being "threshers," are spirits that tread or "stomp" on other people. One huge component of deep healing ministry deals with helping people heal from being stomped on as children.

Israel stayed in constant conflict because it failed to conquer the Canaanite nations like God told them to.

Like teenagers who date or hang around the ungodly, the Canaanite nations were constant pricks in Israel's flesh. Canaan is a type of kingdom. Unfortunately, when Joshua led the troops into Canaan, they failed to root out the enemies which robbed them of total victory. Even though the Kingdom of God is within us, many Christians allow things in their lives, including Jebusite, to rob their peace. Far too many put marriages and families in jeopardy because they fail to conquer condemning Jebusite behaviors like lust, anger, pornography, addictive behaviors and the like.

God gave a promise and a warning before Israel encountered the Jebusites.

📖 My angel will go ahead of you and bring you into the land of the . . . Jebusites, and I will wipe them out. <u>Do not bow down before their gods or worship them or follow their practices</u>. You must <u>demolish them and break their sacred stones to pieces</u>. Worship the Lord your God, and his blessing will be on your food and water. <u>I will take away sickness from among you, and none will miscarry or be barren in your land</u>, I will give you a full life span. Exodus 23:23-26. ^(Underlined for emphasis)

How many homes are in turmoil because people have not dealt with Jebusite? How many families need to be ruined before we stand up to Jebusite and say "enough?"

We MUST learn how to overcome Jebusite attacks so we can release hope to those held in bondage to destructive behaviors.

I stood by the bed of my mother, who, after forty plus years of addiction, struggled to gasp a breath that wouldn't come. Her lungs were full of cancer caused by years of smoking. Her dreams of retiring with my Dad, traveling, gardening, spending extra time with family, helping with the work of the church were all destroyed by her early death. Did she go to heaven? Yes, she knew Jesus. But she left behind people who loved her. She never completed the good works she would have done for God had she not died such an untimely death. I wish I had known then what I know now about deep healing, deliverance, and spiritual warfare. It is too late for her, but not for others who need now what she needed then.

Many struggle unsuccessfully to get victory over addictions or attitudes that master them. They feel condemned because no matter how hard they try they can't put down the destructive habits that hold them in bondage.

People struggle with things which master them rather than Christ: over-eating, nicotine, alcohol, drugs, pornography, foul mouth, anger, eating disorders, self-defeating attitudes.

Let them learn from the nation of Israel who was commanded to destroy all the wicked nations around them, but left some and ended up being defeated by them. While prayer-walking one morning, I thought of a called and gifted middle-aged man who truly wanted to be a minister. I worked with him, but he ended up giving into his flesh and falling back into fornication. He blamed it on me, saying deliverance doesn't work. He was wrong. Deliverance does work, but it doesn't release one from personal responsibility.

Believers are to work out their own salvation with fear and trembling. Jebusite can be easily cast out, but it must be continually resisted. Deliverance ministry is great, but it will never replace a person's need to war against the flesh and spiritual powers.

Jebusite aspires to rule us. We must resist and overcome!

Take a moment to reflect whether anything, other than Jesus, exercises control over you or your family. Such things become demonic strongholds in our lives. Today, by the blood of Jesus, they are coming down!

The nation of Israel was in constant conflict because it did not conquer the Canaanite nations as God told them to. Those nations were constant pricks in their flesh. Canaan was in the land God promised to Abraham and his descendants. When Joshua led the troops into Canaan, however, they failed to root out the enemies that robbed them of total victory. The kingdom of God is in us, but many Christians have things in their lives that rob their peace, even as the Jebusite curse and spirit do. So, I ask . . .

Who is your master; who rules your family?

If you are controlled, in any part of your life, by someone or something other than Jesus, He is not fully Lord of your life! If you have a habit, an addiction, an attitude, or a behavior Jesus doesn't like, it has become master in that area. I don't say this to make anybody feel worse, but to release hope and determination to overcome all such things through the blood of Jesus.

Anything that masters us BECOMES our master!

People who cannot control their fleshly appetites are mastered by those appetites. Jesus and Paul both address this.

📖 <u>No one can serve two masters</u>; for either he will hate the one and will love the other, or he will hold to the one and despise the other. Ye cannot serve God and mammon. Matthew 6:24 DBY. ^(Underlined for emphasis)

📖 Their destiny is destruction, <u>their god is their stomach</u>, and their glory is in their shame. Their mind is set on earthly things. Philippians 3:19 NIV. ^(Underlined for emphasis)

Many lovely Christians sincerely want to serve Jesus, but have one or two hidden sins which keep them from blossoming as disciples. In their hearts, they know what they are doing is wrong, or are convicted about not doing what they should be doing. They know if Jesus were Lord of all, they would overcome those secret sins of commission or omission. They must break every Jebusite hold to come to full repentance!

No amount of self-discipline will break demonic sin patterns. When it is the flesh you can discipline it, but if a demonic stronghold, it must be demolished.

Hosea 4:6 says God's people are destroyed for lack of knowledge. Lack of knowledge concerning spiritual battles, like those in 2 Corinthians 4:4 and 10:3-5, bring destruction. Lack of knowledge concerning spiritual warfare, curses, and the enemies we face destroy many Christians, even as Israel fell repeatedly for the same reason. Such failure brings condemnation, which plays into Jebusite's scheme.

Addressing Condemnation:

The word Jebusite means "treading or trodden down." The root means to tread down with the foot, to pollute and to defile. This spirit brings condemnation, accusation, and intimidation. It treads down, pollutes, and defiles the child of God.

Jebusite endeavors to hold people in bondage through condemnation.

Feelings of condemnation are tough to deal with when one is bound by negative behavior. We have worked with hundreds who struggle with a besetting sin in a sin/confess/sin/confess cycle. They were trodden down. They felt condemned, polluted, and defiled. They felt powerless to change.

A first step to healing and freedom from addiction is breaking strongholds of shame and condemnation. If you don't think you can do it, you won't be able too. If all you can see is your history of failed attempts, you will see yourself as condemned and powerless. But that isn't what the Word of God teaches. The truth will set you free!

Guilt says "I did something bad," shame says "I Am bad."

Self-image has much to do with victory or failure. If we're convinced we are sinners destined to fall, we will. If we realize we are forgiven and as saints and beloved children are destined to godliness, we become increasingly like Jesus. The spirit of the world says "You blew it; you will never get any better." The Spirit of Christ says, "Neither do I condemn thee, go and sin no more" (John 8:11).

Jesus is not in the condemning business, He's in salvage! Better than any American Picker, He sees value in people that others miss. He can take any old wreck and restore it from the inside out -- and has the resources to do so! That is what walking into the Promise Land is all about.

We can sing "Victory in Jesus, my savior forever," but victory is evasive when we listen to the condemning lies of the Accuser. That is why we use scriptural authority to remit people of sin when they confess it (see John 20:23). Romans 8:1 says there is now no condemnation for those who are in Christ Jesus. We need to break shame and condemnation off people and release hope that will not disappoint (Romans 5:5).

Searching for Lost Peace.

If you were saved as an adult, you may remember the peace overflowing your soul when you were born again. I do. On March 17, 1972 at a Bill Gothard seminar, I finally understood what salvation by faith really meant. That night, after months of trying to be a Christian, I simply put my trust in Jesus and asked him to come into my life as Savior and Lord. I remember the truth I used in one of my very first sermons:

📖 Therefore, since we have been justified through faith, we have peace with God through our Lord Jesus Christ. Romans 5:1 NIV.

That was so long ago that I illustrated it with the lingo and finger illustrations of the day. There is one way (finger pointed upward) to peace (peace symbol) through the power (clenched fist) of the cross (fingers crossed).

Like the nation of Israel discovered, I learned I had to resist the devil or peace like a river would not keep on flooding my soul.

The devil robs our peace by holding us in bondage to lusts of the flesh.

The story of Melchizedek the King of Salem is a sad illustration of this.

📖 Then Melchizedek king of Salem (Jerusalem) brought out bread and wine. He was priest of God Most High, and he blessed Abram, saying, "Blessed be Abram by God Most High, Creator of heaven and earth. And blessed be God Most High, <u>who delivered your enemies into your hand</u>." Then Abram gave him a tenth of everything. The king of Sodom said to Abram, "Give me the people and keep the goods for yourself." But Abram said to the king of Sodom, "I have raised my hand to the LORD, God Most High, Creator of heaven and earth, and have taken an oath . . ." Genesis 14:18-20 NIV. (Underlined for emphasis)

Abram and his family were blessed when the King of Salem ruled Jerusalem. But this ancient city's name was changed by King Adoni-Zedek whose name meant "the lord of righteousness." But this king was a son of the devil who sat himself up as lord. He was a Jebusite. He defiled the holy place God set to be his resting place. The heavenly city Jerusalem is a type of our bodies which a temple of the Holy Spirit.

Christians are the temple of the Holy Spirit, yet we still battle with the Jebusite spirit that tries to destroy our bodies which are the temple of the living God. When Jebusite wins, it brings bondage, cancers, sickness, and all sorts of diseases to try to destroy our temples.

📖 Do you not know that your body is a temple of the Holy Spirit, who is in you, whom you have received from God? <u>You are not your own</u>. 1 Corinthians 6:19 NIV. (Underlined for emphasis)

I remember a cartoon where Lucy was chowing down one chocolate after another. Linus asked "Don't you know your body is the temple of the Holy Spirit?" Lucy answered, "Yes, I am trying to make mine a cathedral." I don't think she understood how Jebusite works. I realize food addiction is among the toughest to break, for food is essential to life!

Harold Dewberry, who first introduced me to the Canaanite spirits, gave an example of being bound by a sickness of his son's. It was a Jebusite spirit trying to lord it over their lives, by lording it over their son. Others may be bound by habits: nicotine, alcohol, drugs, immorality, pornography, etc. This is often the work of a Jebusite spirit ruling over them. If it is rules over a Christian's body, it rules over the temple of God! This spirit is after our bodies. If it can affect our bodies, it will control our souls. If we lose the battle, we lose our peace, and begin to feel defiled, trodden down, walked on. We can, we must, overcome every attack against the temple of the Holy Spirit. We must abstain from sin!

📖 Dear friends, I urge you, as aliens and strangers in the world, to abstain from sinful desires, which war against your soul. 1 Peter 2:11 NIV.

Jebusite curses and spirits are seldom mastered in secret.

Pride, condemnation, and fear of rejection are tools Satan uses to hinder Christians, especially Christian leaders, from seeking the very help they need. I love testimonies from pastors and other high-level leaders who risk exposure by filling out a deep healing questionnaire and being transparent in deliverance appointments. There is a reason James 5:16 tells us to confess our faults to one another. I address this need deeply in my book *Getting to the Dirty Rotten Inner Core.*[2]

Every Christian is called to restore those caught in Jebusite strongholds.

We are all called to correct one another in love and in a spirit of humility, brokenness, and mercy. We cannot judge others or we will be judged. We should not criticize a weaker member, because God gives them the greater honor. If we criticize them we may fall into the same behavior. We must not just look at a behavior, but look at the person and see why they are the way they are. I love how The Message tells us to do this.

> 📖 Live creatively, friends. <u>If someone falls into sin, forgivingly restore him</u>, saving your critical comments for yourself. You might be needing forgiveness before the day's out. Stoop down and reach out to those who are oppressed. Share their burdens, and so complete Christ's law. If you think you are too good for that, you are badly deceived. Galatians 6:1-3 MSG. (Underlined for emphasis)

This teaching has exposed a very subtle enemy warring against us. This Jebusite spirit tries to defile our bodies and destroy our families. It is time to bring it down! Consider some indicators Jebusite is working to kill, steal, and destroy you and/or your family.

Indicators Jebusite is at work:
- ☐ Feeling trodden down to defeat.
- ☐ Being held captive to condemnation, defilement or defeat.
- ☐ Continually grieving over past weaknesses and failures.
- ☐ Wearing a cloak of shame, condemnation, or reproach.
- ☐ Feeling people "walk on you."
- ☐ Feeling you have a right to "walk on others."
- ☐ Feeling "less than" or "better than" others.
- ☐ Feeling great distinction between clergy and laity.

- ☐ Feeling "pushed down" rather than edified by others.
- ☐ Feeling greatly discouraged.
- ☐ Struggling with legalism, racism, or class distinction.
- ☐ Struggling with rejection in the context of family, especially from father or mother or spouse.
- ☐ Past abortions.
- ☐ Inability to break powers of addiction.
- ☐ Wearing a cloak of shame, even after sin is confessed and forgiven by God.
- ☐ Personal or ancestral sexual deviance.

BREAKING JEBUSITE CURSES/SPIRITS:

- ⸗ Heavenly Father, in Jesus' Name and through His blood, we confess and repent of every way we and our ancestors have cooperated with Jebusite curses and spirits.
- ⸗ Father, we confess and repent of everywhere we and our ancestors have not loved and followed Your mandate for marriage and family.
- ⸗ We confess and repent of personal and ancestral giving into the work of rejection and self-rejection.
- ⸗ We forgive those who have rejected us and walked on us.
- ⸗ We cast down: defeat, defilement, guilt, shame, condemnation, grief, rejection and self-rejection. (Expel!)
- ⸗ We forgive ourselves for everything God has forgiven us, especially that which built strongholds of shame in our lives.
- ⸗ We tear down every stronghold of shame, bind the strongman of shame, and cast out the spirits and strongman of shame. (Expel!)
- ⸗ We confess letting condemnation work in us and through us.
- ⸗ We break every curse of condemnation and self-condemnation and repent of such behaviors.
- ⸗ We now demolish strongholds and bind strongmen of condemnation and cast down every spirit and strongman of condemnation. (Expel!)
- ⸗ We confess and repent of every place we have given Jebusite to rule or destroy family.
- ⸗ We confess and repent of giving into habits and weaknesses that held us in bondage.
- ⸗ We ask Jesus to reign in our individual bodies, families, and over His church as King of Righteousness and Prince of Peace.

- ⚔ We bind the Jebusite strongman and demolish his stronghold.
- ⚔ In the mighty Name of Jesus, we resist every Jebusite spirit and strongman and cast them down. In Jesus' Name and through His blood we command: Leave us now, and never return! (Expel!)
- ⚔ We will never again be put under your feet!
- ⚔ Father, we ask you to fill us now with your Holy Spirit. (Breathe in His fullness!)
- ⚔ We declare marriage of one man/one woman will again be the foundation of family units.
- ⚔ We pray for our marriages (or singleness) to be healed and restored.
- ⚔ We pray protection from the attack of affairs, addictions, and selfishness.
- ⚔ We pray marriages will stand for sanctity of life, marriage, and religious conviction.
- ⚔ We pray parents will step up as the authority in our homes.
- ⚔ We renounce family curses from our ancestors, and pray blessings upon the next generation. In Jesus' Mighty Name. Amen.

Jebusite addendum on same-gender fornication:

All fornication is sin and weakens marriage relationships.

Christians who lust or engage in pornography or fornication are hypocritical if they judge gays and lesbians. Such a fornicator better take the plank out of his or her own eye before judging same gender fornication. James wrote "For whoever shall keep the whole law, and yet stumble in one point, he is guilty of all" (James 2:10 NKJV). There are times when Christians must judge, but as Jesus said in John 8, "Let him who is without sin cast the first stone." Judging must be done from a position of personal holiness.

Same gender fornication does defile God's wonderful plan of family even more than heterosexual sin.

God ordained family to be comprised of male husbands and female wives, who become parents of sons and daughters. God wants them to live together and advance the Kingdom according to the Biblical mandate for marriage and family.

Jebusite is behind a lot of gender confusion.

Jebusite uses whatever means it can to defile God's plan for marriage and family. It serves its master well by using condemnation to pervert God's intention for men and women.

Baal is king of the Jebusites.

Baal and Jezebel are very similar, but Baal is more encompassing. Jezebel serves Baal. The nations surrounding Israel had their own versions of Baal that were a constant snare to God's people. Baal means "master," "owner," or "lord."

Baal was the god of fertility. Jeremiah 32:35.

Rather than increasing godly seed, Baal destroys children. He is known also as the sun god, the god of provision, the god of rain, and looked to for basically everything. The cult of Baal worship often included male prostitution. Service to the god Molech was also connected with Baal worship, as we can see in Jeremiah:

📖 And they built the high places of Baal which are in the Valley of the Son of Hinnom, <u>to cause their sons and their daughters to pass through the fire to Molech</u>, which I did not command them, nor did it come into My mind that they should do this abomination, to cause Judah to sin. Jeremiah 32:35 NKJV. (Underlined for emphasis)

One serves Baal by serving Molech, the god to whom children were brutally and cruelly sacrificed.

Baal worshippers placed their children in the statue of Molech's red-hot arms and listened to their horrible screams as their child died a horrible torturous demise by burning to death. Have you ever considered that partial birth abortion, or abortion by saline injection is as barbaric for an unborn child as sacrifice to Molech was for an infant?

Baal and Molech are the prevailing gods and influence over abortion.

Since the Roe v. Wade ruling in 1973, more than 59 million babies have been sacrificed at the altar of convenience. During the 2016 United States presidential election, several grumbled there wasn't a better selection of candidates. I couldn't help but wonder if God's intended president had been aborted! Abortion is the ultimate rejection of a child by a parent, evidence that Jebusite is working rejection. The hearts of many are thus turned away, rather than toward their children.

Many consider homosexuality a manifestation of Baal worship.

Male prostitution is integral to Baal ceremonies. Homosexuality is a rejection of one's natural sex drive. This rejection isn't necessarily a conscious choice; but the fruit of rejection sown in a person to defile him. The point is not whether or not one is born homosexual. God's standards of morality are *not* inherent in people by birth. Children must be taught God's standards and adults must choose to abide by them. Few are born with God's standards "bubbling up" in them.

All people are born selfish, and must be trained out of selfishness. God's still working on me in that area, how about you? Selfishness leads to anger, sadness, jealousy, vengeance, and cruelty. These inherent feelings must be corrected by conforming to God's higher authority of morality. All the descriptions of love in 1 Corinthians 13 are anti-natural. People do not naturally want to "bear with, believe, forgive, endure, think no wrong, etc."

Why do we deify "natural" sexual drive as God-ordained?

It isn't. None of us, heterosexual or homosexual, is born with a monogamous sex drive, but that doesn't justify fornication or adultery. Some apparently think they are "born" with feelings toward pedophilia or even bestiality. If, as many assume, a sex drive is self-validating, we quickly stray into apostasy.

Demons are on assignment to warp our sexual identities when we are young, so we'll have inordinate and confused sex drives. Studies show most porn stars and strip club dancers were sexually abused by close male figures when they were young. That's also true for a high percentage of homosexuals. This is tragic, but is certainly not reason to validate sexual deviance.

If we demolish Jebusite's strongholds, God will release new levels of power for healing and restoration!

I am very aware how many have struggled with homosexual feelings and cried out to God to take them away. I grieve over teens and young adults I've ministered to who struggle with such things. The church can defeat Jebusite and when it does, it will receive power to set people free from all Jebusite's tools to destroy marriage and family.

Prayer for anointing to share the love of God with others.

- Heavenly Father, we confess every way we and our ancestors have sinned by directly or indirectly participating with Baal, Molech, Jebusite, or any other god coming against Your plan for marriage and family.
- In Jesus' Name, we ask you to break every hold of Baal, Molech, Jebusite or any other god over us, our families, and church.
- We command these powers and principalities to loose us and go now! (expel)
- Lord of heaven, there is no stronghold or demon that can stand up to You, or to Your church when it operates in Your authority.
- Equip me, Father, with the love of Jesus to meet people where they are, accept them as they are, but pull them into Your love which will free them to be all You created them to be.
- Forgive me for every judgmental attitude and for being more concerned about being "right" than loving people.
- Equip my hands for war and help me tear down Jebusite strongholds for family members, and in my city, state, and nations.
- Father, restore Your church to power, and guide Your church in restoring families to Your good and life-giving model.
- In Jesus' Name, amen.

Endnotes:

[1]*The Seven Mountain Prophecy* – Johnny Enlow – Summary Sheet. http://www.the7mountains.com/2010/01/24/the-seven-mountain-prophecy-johnny-enlow-summary-sheet/
[2]*Getting to the Dirty Rotten Inner Core*, Doug Carr, Create Space, 2014.

Further Information on Jebusite.

[1]http://app.razorplanet.com/acct/41587-1571/resources/WC...The_Jebusite_Spirit.doc
[2]http://shamah-elim.info/jebusite.htm
[3]http://www.7culturalmountains.org/apps/articles/default.asp?articl eid=39120&columnid=4335

5 HITTITE

What does perfect love cast out? God's word says "perfect love casts out fear!" (1 John 4:8)

Hittite is a misleading influence or powerful delusion that makes people believe *THE* LIE.

📖 And for this reason God sends them a misleading influence that they <u>may believe the lie</u>. 2 Thessalonians 2:11 WEY. ^{(Underlined for} emphasis)

The lie leads us to fear that God isn't here, (or wasn't there), or doesn't care.

Second Thessalonians 2:1-12 speaks of the coming of the man of lawlessness at the time of the Anti-Christ. God sends them the delusion or misleading influence that they *may* (not *will*) believe the lie. Those who "believe the lie" are people who refuse to love the truth and be saved. Still, this warning is given to Christians so they will not be deceived in any way, because the secret power of lawlessness is already at work.

The devil strength is lies; he uses fear which denies God's love, and present concern for people.

We talked about Amorite. Words have the power to bless or curse, especially words spoken against people. We've discussed Jebusite, and how it purposes to make us feel trodden down, polluted, defiled and condemned. We will also deal with the Canaanite spirit that brings us down through trafficking or trade.

Johnny Enlow summarizes the seven Canaanite spirits and their place of attack on the Seven Mountains. He says Hittites (represent bad news) are the Enemy of the mountain of Media. They work under the principality Apollyon (destroyer) to displace the significant authority of Evangelists to fill the airways with "good news" to bring the Revelation 5:12 Key: Blessing.[1]

Hittite means a fright, dread, made afraid, scared, terrified, broken, and amazed.

The Hittites were one of the first enemies the Israelites encountered when they entered the land of Canaan. That gives a pattern or example to keep us from setting our hearts on evil things as they did. One of the first enemies we must overcome is fear, not fear of the Lord, but dread that causes us to be fearful and scared. Fear will stop us from inheriting the fullness of God's blessing, and from bringing Good News to the media. Fear is very strange and we can be afraid of a lot of things. That is why the enemy tries to keep us in bondage to fear. When we accept the truth about ourselves and who we are in Jesus, His truth liberates us and sets us free.

📖 Then you will know the truth, and the truth will set you free. John 8:32 NIV.

Satan is the Father of lies. He began his work in people when he lied to Adam and Eve, and tries the same with you and me. I used to be in bondage to fears that would have kept me from fulfilling God's will, had the spirit of fear not been broken off.

Fear of public speaking.

I was so afraid of public speaking I skipped class whenever I was to give a speech. I used to get sick just at the thought of going up in front of people. I got so sick my parents had to take me home from a 4-H banquet because I was supposed to go up front to receive a reward. Satan knew God would call me to preach and tried to use this fear to keep me from answering God's call.

Fear of people's opinions.

I greatly feared what people thought of me. I was afraid I would do something stupid and people would see me, so I hesitated to even sing in public. I also feared I might do something right and people wouldn't like it. Such fear kept me from trying. I was so afraid of failing I wouldn't risk anything. I learned the hard way you can't lead a church by public opinion. You have to hear from God and follow him. I couldn't do that while I was captive to the fear of what people thought of me.

Fear of lack.

I feared not making it financially. I thought I had to have a good paying job and know where every week's check was coming from. Had I not been delivered from that spirit of fear, I never would have given up my good paying job to go to college and enter the ministry. Fear almost kept me from preparing for the work God called me to. Don't let that happen to you. Let me share several examples of fear at work from the Bible.

Adam and Eve - the first humans bound by fear.

Fear is first found in Genesis 3:10.

He answered, "I heard you in the garden, and <u>I was afraid</u> because I was naked; so I hid." Genesis 3:10 NIV. (Underlined for emphasis)

God never did anything to make Adam and Eve afraid of Him. He loved them, and walked with them. Even after they ate the forbidden fruit, God looked for them, not to punish them, but to protect them. Even after their sin, He wanted to bless them with a cloak of skin. That was when the first promise of Jesus was given.

Adam and Eve were so afraid of God, they wanted to hide from Him. Have you ever done that? It may be Hittite at work.

Abraham - the father of faith - failed because of fear.

Abraham is the Old Testament prototype of faith. He believed God and it was credited to him as righteousness. But this dear man of faith put his wife at risk because of fear. In Genesis 12:10-20, for example, Abram was afraid of being murdered so people could take advantage of his beautiful wife. He believed the lie God wouldn't protect him or his wife, so he asked her to lie to Pharaoh and claim to be his sister. Why did this great man of faith treat his wife the way he did? It was fear that caused him to trust in deception rather than trust God to protect their lives. Isn't that what happens every time someone tells a lie to save their own skin?

Peter's fear made him revert to his old ways.

Peter is one of my favorite Bible characters. He was impulsive and ready to give it his all. He stood against the soldiers and cut one of their ears off. He was always ready for a good fight. But Peter learned about fear the hard way. His fear made him deny Jesus and almost destroyed him. It was Peter's fear that drove him back to his boats after the betrayal, arrest, and crucifixion of Jesus. Fear was still present after Jesus rose from the dead. Peter saw Jesus, but feared Jesus could never love him again. He went back to his old trade of fishing. That is where Jesus found him in John 21. Jesus had already appeared to the disciples, but this time they are fishing and Jesus tells them to cast the net out again even though the fishing had stunk. They did, caught a huge mess of fish, and Peter jumped overboard to greet Jesus.

Faith helped Peter out of the boat; fear drove him back into the boat. (Matthew 14:25-31)

Jesus' response to Peter when he began to sink was "You of little faith, "why did you doubt?" The disciples freaked out when they saw Jesus walking on the water. Jesus immediately said: "Take courage! It is I. Don't be afraid." Don't judge Peter, at least he got out of the boat! It is easier to trust God when you are safe in the boat, than when you are caught in the storm. Peter did alright as long as he kept his eyes on Jesus. But when he heard the roar of the wind and saw the power of the waves, he began to sink.

Perfect love casts out fear – IF we receive it. (John 21:15-19)

Fear of God's rejection keeps us from loving union with the Father. Perfect love begins with God's Agape love, in which there is no variation or shadow. Peter's love was so shallow that when Jesus asked Peter if he loved him with Agape love (perfect love), all Peter could say was he loved him with phileo (brotherly love). Jesus loved Peter perfectly, but Peter had a hard time believing it. He was so focused on his failures he couldn't see God's love, acceptance, and forgiveness.

Fear of suffering.

Evidently Peter feared crucifixion. He witnessed the horror of Jesus' death on the cross. He watched as Jesus gasped His last breath.

He saw the agony. When Peter went back his boat, he ran in fear Pharisees, who might also kill him. In John 21:9 Jesus indicated what kind of death Peter would die and commanded him to "Glorify God." Jesus told him to face his fear, take up his cross, and follow.

Peter never shrank away from Jesus again. He made some mistakes, but never the mistake of not loving Jesus enough to die for him. Peter later was crucified because he refused to quit preaching Jesus. Tradition has it that Peter asked to be crucified upside down because he didn't feel worthy of dying like Jesus did. Peter came to know God's perfect love drives out fear and enables you to risk doing and being what God created you to do and be.

Fear of having to do more than others. (John 21:21-23)

Peter's main concern after Jesus let him know how he was to die was: "What about John?" I mean, it's ok I have to pay a price, but I don't want to be the only one who does so. I understand his thinking. I was once asked by an elder to take a 50% cut in pay. At the time, I was hurt. I was willing to, but only if all the elders would do the same thing. Yes, I did repent and there have been times when I've received a 100% cut without complaining. I had to learn what Peter learned. Jesus told him it wasn't any of his business what happened to John. He looked Peter square in the eye and said "you must follow me."

Improper fear of the Lord.

I feared the Lord improperly until 1990. I had been a successful Youth for Christ worker for three years and pastor for twelve years. I still feared God, however, not in the fear of the Lord is the beginning of wisdom sense, but in the "I'm not going to do enough or I'm going to mess up and God won't love me anymore" sense. Then, after the worst period of my life, God proved He loved me still, not because I was good or because I measured up, but because His love is measureless. I finally learned God loves me unconditionally because He is good, not *if* I am good. He loves me perfectly, not based on my merit but on His attributes of love. I learned I couldn't work hard and make him love me more, and I couldn't mess up and make Him love me less. Finally, I allowed His perfect love drove out my fear. Hittite lost its hold, and I quit believing the lie I had to earn God's love by never failing. "Fear Not" is used over 300 times in the Bible. Jesus used it. The Old Testament used it repeatedly. What are some of things people fear? One section of our Deep Healing Questionnaire deals lists following fears.

Fear of: failure; inability to cope; inadequacy; death; authority figures; the dark; violence; rape; being alone; Satan and evil spirits; the future; women; grocery stores; heights; insanity; men; public speaking; people's opinions; accident; old age; enclosed places; terminal illness; breakup; insects; divorce or marriage; spiders; dogs; snakes; animals; loud noises; water; pain; flying in an airplane; open spaces; crowds; and death or injury of a loved one. Christians often circle 50 - 80% of these. I am talking about good Christians who are gripped by fear. Fears like these give evidence of the Hittite spirit at work. When we are afraid, we can take notice from Job.

How Job's fear came to fruition.

📖 <u>What I feared</u> has come upon me; <u>what I dreaded</u> has happened to me. Job 3:25 NIV. ^(Underlined for emphasis)

This is powerful. Job recognized it when his fears and dreads manifested. This still happens. People who fear getting cancer, or in an accident often do! God gave Satan permission to do what he did to Job, but I think God saw Job's fear, and granted Satan permission to attack, so He proved once for all that perfect love casts out fear.

Fear reaps the folly of specific fears.
Faith reaps the fullness of God's blessings.

Timothy's temptation to fear of ministry.

Timothy filled in for Paul, who was in prison. His best friend and mentor was on death row. Those out to get Paul would soon be after Timothy. Fear of what people might do or say hinders us from fulfilling God's purpose in and through our lives. Ministry can be scary! We must not give into fear of being rejected or hurt by people. Fear of rejection keeps us from sharing Christ and from being transparent with other. Timothy wrestled with such fears, so Paul encouraged Timothy to be bold for Jesus.

📖 For this reason I remind you to fan into flame the gift of God, which is in you through the laying on of my hands. For <u>God did</u>

<u>not give us a spirit of timidity</u>, but a spirit of power, of love and of self-discipline. 2 Timothy 1:6-7 NIV. <small>(Underlined for emphasis)</small>

Fear of rejection keeps people from sharing their needs with one another, which is a major reason so many lack wholeness. It is sad how few call for the elders to pray over them and heal them when they are sick. Some are afraid to admit they have a need because they fear what others might think.

Some fear they will be a bother, or fear they might be rejected or turned down if they call. If we do not acknowledge our fears, we will be held in captivity. Jacob illustrates this. After he wrestled with God, the angel asked "what is your name," and Jacob confessed "thief, twister and supplanter." Once Jacob acknowledged his condition, God said "no longer, now you will be called Israel-- one who strives with God and overcomes." Isn't that what you want to be -- one who overcomes fear and walks with God?

The basis of revival is vulnerability – not fear!

See if you recognize any of them in yourself in any of the following fears:

Do you fear you are guilty before God?

Guilt is not an emotion, but a standing before God. We are either guilty or not guilty. If we consider ourselves to be guilty (when we are under the blood of Jesus) we are saying, we are under God's condemnation and judgment. The Bible says "if we have been washed in the blood there is no condemnation and we have passed out of condemnation into life." If you are cleansed by the blood of Jesus and still fear being guilty, the Hittite spirit is at work.

Do you fear God wants to punish you?

What causes people to be afraid of God? They may fear God will punish them, perhaps like their earthly father did. I only received one spanking in my life that I didn't deserve. My alcoholic Grandfather dragged me to the river, even though Dad said I couldn't go to the river. Dad noticed I was missing, ran to the river in fear, and saw me there with Grandpa. I was whipped every step of the way home. I came to wrongly view God that way. God is Love! Consider what the Scripture says:

📖 If anyone acknowledges that Jesus is the Son of God, God lives in him and he in God. And <u>so we know and rely on the love God has for us</u>. God is love. Whoever lives in love lives in God, and God in him. In this way, love is made complete among us so that we will have confidence on the day of judgment, because in this world we are like him. <u>There is no fear in love</u>. But perfect love drives out fear, because <u>fear has to do with punishment</u>. The one who fears is not made perfect in love.1 John 4: 15-18 NIV. (Underlined for emphasis)

You may wonder: "What about responsibility for my behavior?" Yes, God holds us responsible, but God does so with redeeming love. He is not here to condemn us or cast us out. There is no judgment in those who are in Christ Jesus.

Do you fear condemnation?

Spirits of condemnation work with Hittite to keep people in bondage so they will never fulfill their destinies, regardless how hard they try. Fear makes people thrive in life and ministry, but faith helps us to thrive. We don't bear fruit by working hard or beating our bodies into submission. We bear fruit and thrive by abiding in the vine. Fear of condemnation hinders us from doing so. Grab the truth of the following passages and cast out condemnation forever!

📖 For just as the Father raises the dead and gives them life, even so the Son gives life to whom he is pleased to give it. Moreover, the Father judges no one, but has entrusted all judgment to the Son, that all may honor the Son just as they honor the Father. He who does not honor the Son does not honor the Father, who sent him. "I tell you the truth, <u>whoever hears my word and believes him who sent me has eternal life and **will not be condemned**</u>; he has crossed over from death to life." John 5:21-24 NIV. (Underlined and bold font for emphasis)

📖 Therefore, <u>there is now no condemnation for those who are in Christ Jesus</u>, because through Christ Jesus the law of the Spirit of life set me free from the law of sin and death. For what the law was powerless to do in that it was weakened by the sinful nature, God did by sending his own Son in the likeness of sinful man to be a sin offering. And so he condemned sin in sinful man, in order that the righteous requirements of the law might be fully met in us, who do not live according to the sinful nature but according to the Spirit. Romans 8:1-4 NIV. (Underlined for emphasis)

Do you fear you are not God's child or that He does not want to father you?

I recently did ministry with a wonderful man of God. He had endured a rough childhood, a father who left him behind, a mother who was so crushed she didn't know what to do. Some of his life experiences made him fear God didn't love him. Though he is a wonderful pastor and leader, he led out of compassion rather than from the Father's love. He was actually hooting and hollering after he realized God had never left him nor forsaken him. He was overcome with joy God is a good - good father and he is loved by him! He finally accepted for himself what he preached to others for years.

Do you fear you will be separated from God's love?

I was a religious workaholic for the first 20 years of my Christian life! I feared I somehow had to earn God's love, acceptance, and forgiveness. Every time I messed up I feared I would lose any love He might have for me. I knew the Scriptures in my head, but not in my heart.

For you did not receive a spirit that makes you a slave again to fear, but you received the Spirit of sonship. And by him we cry, "Abba, Father." The Spirit himself testifies with our spirit that we are God's children. Now if we are children, then we are heirs--heirs of God and co-heirs with Christ, if indeed we share in his sufferings in order that we may also share in his glory. Romans 8:15-17 NIV. (Underlined for emphasis)

People get caught in the lie God doesn't love them because of what their parents did to them. God's love is about what people did to us. We see God's love through His sacrificial gift of His son to purchase our redemption. For those God foreknew he also predestined to be conformed to the likeness of his Son, that he might be the firstborn among many brothers. And those he predestined, he also called; those he called, he also justified; those he justified, he also glorified. What, then, shall we say in response to this? <u>If God is for us, who can be against us</u>? He who did not spare his own Son, but gave him up for us all--how will he not also, along with him, graciously give us all things? Who will bring any charge against those whom God has chosen? It is God who justifies Who is he that condemns? Christ Jesus, who died--more than that, who was raised to life--is at the right hand of God and is also interceding for us Who shall separate us from the love of Christ? Shall trouble or hardship or persecution or famine or nakedness or danger or sword? As it is written: "For your sake we face death all day long; we are considered as sheep to be slaughtered." No, in all these things we are more than conquerors through him who loved us. <u>For I am convinced that</u> neither death nor life, neither angels nor demons, neither the present nor the future, nor any powers, neither height nor depth, nor anything else in all creation, <u>will be able to separate us from the love of God that is in Christ Jesus our Lord</u>. Romans 8:29-39 NIV ^(Underlined for emphasis)

I've heard this paraphrased: "If God so be for us, everyone else may as well be!"

Do you fear trying or do you fear failure?

Remember the man who hid talent because he was afraid? He wasn't free to become all he could be. He was a slave because anyone who fears is a slave to fear. The Hittite spirit wants to cause us to be afraid and he creates situations to cause us to be afraid. He tried that with me when I entered the ministry in 1973 and when I reentered the ministry in 1992. My fear of being hurt or messing up again almost kept me from being a pastor.

If you sense God calling you to do certain things for Him, but hesitate because of fear, Hittite is at work.
Do you fear terrorism or catastrophe?

The 9/11/2001 terrorist attack did something to Americans. Even children and teenagers who weren't alive then, feel the work of fear working through others who witnessed planes crashing into the Twin Towers. The goal of terrorists is to drive us mad with terror. They want to make us afraid to go to work, school, to the mall, or even to church. I remember how fearful my dad became whenever I went to other nations to minister. He feared something would happen when

I went to Mexico, Namibia, and India. He couldn't understand what God has taught me.

**The safest place to be is in
the center of God's will!**

Common manifestations of Hittite:

- ☐ Fears-phobias
- ☐ Panic attacks
- ☐ Heart attacks
- ☐ Torment-horror
- ☐ Trauma (past or present)
- ☐ Nightmares-terror
- ☐ Anxiety-stress
- ☐ Doubt and unbelief
- ☐ Worry
- ☐ Hyper-tension
- ☐ Fretting; etc.
- ☐ Condemnation.

The following come from an internet article on Hittite spirits from Razor Planet.[2]

Hittite can be found in those who practice:

- ☐ Gossip and slander
- ☐ Those who abuse others by use of words and speech
- ☐ Inordinate desire to keep secrets
- ☐ Those who terrorize others in whatever form it may take
- ☐ Rumor-starters who delight to instill fear and distress others
- ☐ Leaders who quench the Holy Spirit's voice
- ☐ Those who try to discourage instead of encourage
- ☐ Undue criticism bent on controlling others

Hittite may be present those who suffer from:

- ☐ Phobias of all kinds
- ☐ Fear and mental torments
- ☐ Those who are melancholy in nature (a feeling of thoughtful sadness)
- ☐ Ongoing suicidal tendencies
- ☐ Long-term depression
- ☐ Irresponsibility and un-accountability
- ☐ Co-dependence on others as a way of escape[3]

How to deal with fear:

Confess fear.

Don't afraid to confess your fear. Confess you lack enough knowledge of God's love to "fear not." Ask God to fill your heart with His perfect love. Ask Him to shed His love abroad in your heart and give you perfect love that casts out fear. Stir up the gift that is in you (the gift of the Holy Spirit).

You have power, glory to God. You have the Holy Spirit in you and He is greater than any fear you will ever face!

Renounce fear.

Fear is your enemy, not your friend. Resist it and it will flee!

Breaking Hittite curses and resisting Hittite spirits:

- Father, we confess and repent of every wicked thing we or our ancestors have put before our eyes.
- We confess and repent of the hold media has had on our hearts, minds and spirits.
- We forgive those who have brought terror, dread, and fear into our lives.
- We confess and repent of where we and our ancestors have given into fear and terror.
- We confess and repent of every place we, or our ancestors, gave place to Hittite curses, strongholds, or demons.
- We repent of personal and ancestral agreement with fear and any Hittite curse or spirit.

We cast down:

- Spirits of fear and terror. (Expel!)
- Every demon that has attached through media. (Expel!)
- We bind the Hittite strongman and destroy its stronghold.
- We now command every Hittite spirit to loose us now. (Expel!)
- Apollyon, you destroyer, release me now and take your curses of destruction with you! (Expel!)
- We break your assignments and command your servants to go to the feet of Jesus.
- We bind you, Hittite strongman, and command you to leave. NOW! In Jesus' name. (Expel)

꜓ Father, we ask you to fill us with Your Spirit.
꜓ We receive Your perfect love which casts out fear.
꜓ We declare You have not given us the spirit of fear, but of power, and of love, and of a sound mind! (2 Timothy 1:7)

Endnotes:

[1] From: The Seven Mountain Prophecy – Johnny Enlow – Summary Sheet. http://www.the7mountains.com/2010/01/24/the-seven-mountain-prophecy-johnny-enlow-summary-sheet/

[2] The HITTITE Spirit/ "Spirits of Fear, Terror, and discouragement." http://app.razorplanet.com/acct/41587-1571/resources/WC...The_HITTITE_Spirit.doc

References for further study:

1) PRAYER AGAINST THE SPIRITS OF FEAR. March 2, 2013 at 2:16pm, SPIRIT OF FEAR (HITTITE SPIRIT). http://www.facebook.com/notes/grace-elizabeth-joy-anderson/prayer-against-the-spirit-of-fear/497374913631944

2) Shamah-Elim, The Hittites First posted: June 19, 2004. http://shamah-elim.info/hittite.htm

6 CANAANITE

The Canaanites (represent love of money, mammon and greed) work in the mountain of Business and Commerce under the direction of Mammon (greed).

Johnny Enlow shares how the Canaanites (representing love of money) are the Enemy of the Mountain of Economy. They work under the principality Mammon (greed) to displace the significant authority of prophets who have the basic mission to discover and transfer wealth into kingdom purposes. Revelation 5:12 Key: Wealth.[1]

Money is not evil, but the love of money is the root of all evil (1 Timothy 6:10). Babylon is a primary example of Canaanite and may be a strongman in partnership with Canaanite. The meaning of the word Canaanite is: "to be brought low by traffic or trade" (personal business dealings). Canaanite affects our trading or our trafficking in money and causes us to covet after things, and holds us in captivity and bondage through finances.

It is tragic to see people, whether married or single, young or old, who are in such financial bondage they live from pay check to pay check. If they are injured or sick for more than a few days, they might lose everything they have! It is troubling how many good, hard working people end up in bankruptcy. God calls us to be financially free so we can live like He wants us to live and give like He wants us to give. God wants his people to have enough money for their own need, plus help meet the needs of the poor and down trodden.

We need to carefully consider how to break the power of the Canaanite curse and spirit which keeps families, churches, states and nations in such troubled states of finances they cannot seem to raise their heads above water.

EXAMPLES OF CANAANITE AT WORK:

How Achan's greed killed him. (Joshua 7)

Achan's sin proves greed can lead to early death. You probably remember how Jericho was tightly shut up because of the Israelites. God told

Israel to be silent and march around the city once a day for six days. On the seventh day, they marched around the city seven times and when the trumpets sounded, the walls came tumbling down, and the army went in and overthrew the city.

How much sense did it make for the Israelites to march around the city several times while on a forced word fast? Without a doubt, some of them thought Joshua was crazy, but God works in mysterious ways. Even when it comes to financial freedom, giving to gain, or breaking curses to step into blessing, or dealing with strongmen like Canaanite and/or Babylon may seem crazy! Before they went in, Joshua said:

📖 Keep away from the devoted things, <u>so that you will not bring about your own destruction by taking any of them.</u> Otherwise you will make the camp of Israel liable to destruction and bring trouble on it. Joshua 6:18 NIV. (Underlined for emphasis)

Achan, however, thought he could get away with ignoring the Lord's commands. He thought they applied to everyone except him. He was tempted by some of the goods and slipped some things into a secret place. He tried to get away with having things God didn't want him to have, but his sin brought defeat to everyone! The Lord was angry and Israel was defeated in a very easy battle.

When Canaanite is at work it affects entire families, churches, and governments. When Israel sought the Lord to find out why they were defeated, He pointed out there was sin in the camp! They soon discovered what Achan had done, and he was put to death for bringing destruction on the camp because of his greedy, covetous ways.

How many families do you know which have been or are being destroyed over money issues? The New York Times shared an article Money Fights Predict Divorce Rates.[2]

You know it in your gut, and you've seen it in the splintered marriages around you. Finance-related tensions — however you define them — raise the risk of divorce.

A new study, by Jeffrey Dew at Utah State University, attempts to quantify that risk. His finding: Couples who reported disagreeing about finance once a week were over 30 percent more likely to get divorced than couples who reported disagreeing about finances a few times a month.

Professor Dew looked at responses from about 2,800 couples surveyed in 1987 by the National Survey of Families and Households. In this survey, both husbands and wives were asked, separately, about how often they disagreed with their spouse over chores, in-laws, spending time together, sex and money. These same respondents were then contacted again several years later, in 1992, and asked if they were still married.

Of all these common things couples fight about, money disputes were the best harbingers of divorce. For wives, disagreements over finances and sex were good predictors of divorce, but finance disputes were much stronger predictors. For husbands, financial disagreements were the only type of common disagreement that predicted whether they would get a divorce.[2]

The American way is to buy every little thing our hearts desire, regardless of need or ability to pay. Just think of Black Friday shopping and the Christmas craze. Many end up in such financial stress they can't afford vacations, can't buy everything they need, and can't support the work of the Lord like they should. Such is the work of Canaanite!

How Gehazi's covetousness clung to him. (2 Kings 5)

Do you remember Namaan who was a commander for the King of Aram? He was a great military leader, and highly respected, but he had leprosy. Namaan's army had taken a young girl captive and she had become the servant of Namaan's wife. The girl did not become bitter, but determined to let God use her right where she was! She told Namaan's wife about the prophet Elisha who could heal Namaan.

Namaan's wife believed the slave girl and convinced her husband to visit Elisha. When Namaan got there, Elisha simply told him to wash himself seven times in the Jordan river. That ticked Namaan off. He didn't travel such a distance to wash in the Jordan river. That didn't make sense! Do you see a pattern here? God often calls us to do things by faith that don't make any sense to us. It didn't make sense to wash in the Jordan. Namaan had bathed regularly at home, but God was up to something. Namaan wanted man to give him what only God could. He expected healing to come in some spectacular way, so he took off in a huff.

Thankfully, one of his servants talked him into cooling down and giving it a try. When Namaan obeyed Elisha's prophetic command and did something as irrational as dipping in the Jordan seven times, he was healed!

Namaan was so grateful he wanted to pay Elisha but Elisha refused any gift and Namaan started home. Refusing payment didn't make sense to Elisha's servant Gehazi. He probably hadn't had a raise for a long time and he knew Namaan could afford to pay a reward. So Gehazi decided to take the reward for himself. He didn't see where it would hurt anybody. After all, Namaan *had* offered money. Elisha didn't want it, but Gehazi did.

Gehazi didn't think anyone would find out, but God revealed his deed to Elisha, who rebuked him and said Namaan's leprosy would cling to him, which it did. Leprosy is an old testament picture of sin. Gehazi's reward for his covetousness was leprosy. Perhaps Canaanite was at work.

Ananias and Sapphira embraced two worlds and lost both.

Ananias and Sapphira were so committed to the church they gave a huge gift of money after they sold some property. They pretended to give their all, but held on to a nest egg--just in case God didn't take care of them. It was their money, and other than the tithe, they could do anything they wanted with it. But they wanted to make it look like they were giving their all and then some, when they were only giving their some (Acts 5:1-11).

Checkbooks are the last thing most people place on the altar, and the first thing they take off. Some pastors monitor their people's giving because it is a sign of spiritual health. I have not done that in the churches I've pastored. I trust I am not being a spiritual wimp, because I agree giving is a huge component of spiritual health.

Few families and ministries would lack if everyone simply tithed. I clearly remember how impossible tithing seemed to me when I was first saved. I was barely making it on a whopping $160.00 a week. I thought I would face bankruptcy if I tithed $16 weekly. For me it became a matter of faith and obedience. Thankfully I learned that before I quit my job to enter ministry at $100.00 a week and go to college. God takes care of our all when we trust him *with* our all.

Can you imagine how we might sing, if like in the movie "Liar, Liar" we couldn't lie:

- I surrender some.
- Take my life and leave me be.
- Just as I pretend to be.
- Jesus paid it all, nothing to him I owe.
- "Interesting Grace"
- "Blessed Hunch"
- "What an Acquaintance We Have in Jesus"

- "My Hope Is Built on Nothing Much"
- "I'm Fairly Certain My Redeemer Lives"
- "Blest Be the Tie that Doesn't Cramp My Style"
- "Oh God Our Enabler in Ages Past"
- "I've Got Peace Like a Trickle"
- "A Comfy Mattress Is Our God"
- "When the Saints Go Sneaking in"

Ananias and Sapphira wanted the best of both worlds. They wanted to look like they trusted God, but they looked out for themselves. They didn't fool God, and they didn't fool Peter. Rather than trusting Jehovah as Jireh, they faced Him as Judge, and it cost them their lives.

Canaanite deals with areas in our lives where we are more concerned about self than the Kingdom.

Selfish independence led Israel to defeat time and again:

Self-preservation.
When times became rough they blamed God. "Why did you bring us into the desert to die?" God wanted the people to learn to trust Him to take care of them. They, however, refused to walk by faith and walked by sight instead.

Material gain.
They asked "Why did you bring us here to destroy our cattle." God wanted them to believe He would provide for them, but they literally placed more trust in their *stocks* (cattle- get it? Pun intended) then they did in Jehovah Jireh, their provider.

Physical appetites.
Israel complained "Our soul loathes this bread." God wanted to teach them to eat to live, but they lived to eat. They were like kids who come home, rummage through stocked cupboards and refrigerators and complain "there's nothing to eat." Translated that means "I want a Twinkie, potato chips, and pop." God wants His children to know life doesn't consist of bread alone.

Spiritual appetites.
God wanted them to love and honor Him alone. But they wanted a god

they could see with their natural eyes, not just their spiritual eyes. They sacrificed their gold so Aaron could make them a golden calf to worship. Think of what most people look for when they begin church shopping. They want the nicest buildings, best children's ministries, and shortest services. How many really care if God is present?

The Canaanite nations represent spiritual forces of evil we must overcome, IF we want to walk in the fullness of God's promises and purposes for our lives. The enemy wants to frustrate us and cause conflict in our lives, so we lose the peace linked to righteousness. If we lose our peace, we lose our power with God. Remember our key verse:

📖 Now these things occurred as examples to keep us from setting our hearts on evil things as they did. Do not be idolaters, as some of them were … 1 Corinthians 10:6-7a NIV.

Canaanite brings destruction when we love Mammon more than God, or handle money in selfish ways rather than God's way.
Jesus said:

📖 No man can serve two masters. Either he will hate the one and love the other, or he will be devoted to the one and despise the other. <u>You cannot serve both God and Money</u>. Matthew 6:24 NIV. (Underlined for emphasis)

Please notice how "Money" is capitalized. The King James more accurately uses the word "Mammon." It too, is capitalized because in the Greek, Mammon is a proper name. Mammon in the Bible does not refer to the currency we use to buy groceries or give offerings. Mammon refers to the god of this world behind the selfish use of money. Money is not the root of all evil; the love of money is. Love of money is hard core idolatry. If we trust God to supply our needs, we will use our money as He directs. If we trust our money and use it however we want, money becomes Mammon with a capital M. It becomes our god and the Canaanite spirit has us.

Lessons from the nation of Canaan:
The word Canaanite means to be brought low by trading or trafficking. It brings us down through misuse of money. When we study the Canaanites as an example to keep us from setting our hearts on evil things, we learn how to avoid the Canaanite spirit. Do you know anyone who has lost their peace and joy over finances, traffic or trade? Have you?

Canaanite makes people and nations targets for fraud.

In 1920, Scotchman Arthur Ferguson, had an amazing selling ability. He went to London and sold Big Ben for $100,000 to a person who had more money than wisdom. Later he sold Buckingham Palace to an unsuspecting victim. Then he came to America and rented the White House to somebody for $100,000 a year, who paid cash in advance. He tried to sell the Statue of Liberty with a $100,000 cash down payment. He told an Australian Tourist the port authority was going to expand the harbor so the statue had to be sold. Unfortunately, the Australian had trouble getting his money through so there was a delay. This delay aggravated Mr. Ferguson, and the tourist became suspicious. Ferguson was finally arrested for fraud and put in prison for five years. He served his term, and was released to enjoy all the money he had gained and lived a life of luxury. He had the Canaanite spirit, but so did the people who wanted to buy things that would never have been for their good.

Things like that never happen to us, do they? While working on this I received a call from a credit card company enticing me to accept an offer of 6% interest. Sounds good, doesn't it? Not to me, I much prefer the zero percent I pay because I pay off my credit cards in full each month. Is it possible Canaanite is working against people caught in credit card debt?

Being brought low by money, traffic, or trade brings dis-appointment.

I used a hyphen to show how money can hinder divine appointment. In the books of Exodus and Joshua, we see how the Lord brought Israel out of Egypt with great signs, wonders, and miracles. He provided for them, and the fear of the Lord came on all the Canaanite nations. But soon the Children of Israel suffered defeat after many great victories. They wondered why the Lord let them down. God allowed them to be tested to see if they would trust God and give Him the glory. God says "All the gold and silver belongs to me" but Achan came under the influence of Canaanite, and lost everything because of it.

Joshua 7 indicates there is nothing wrong with gold and silver, as long as you're not hanging on to what belongs to God. 2 Kings 5 shows there is nothing wrong with receiving pay for working for the Lord, but we can't get caught in the Babylonian garment of the things of this world like Gehazi did. Acts 5 shows how the blessings of God can become a curse when if we put our trust in them, or wrongfully hang on to them. How many people do you know who have come under the grip of financial problems or the lure of riches and slipped away from the Lord?

If we hold onto what belongs to God, it becomes a curse.

Malachi Three states the whole nation of Israel was under a curse because they withheld the tithe from God. Anyone who thinks they are getting ahead by withholding their tithes and offerings are fooling themselves.

True prosperity is a matter of the heart, not the wallet.

Canaanite is out to rob, kill, and destroy by getting us to covet that which is God's, God has a better plan.

> But godliness with contentment is great gain. For we brought nothing into the world, and we can take nothing out of it. But if we have food and clothing, we will be content with that. People who want to get rich fall into temptation and a trap and into many foolish and harmful desires that plunge men into ruin and destruction. For the love of money is a root of all kinds of evil. Some people, eager for money, have wandered from the faith and pierced themselves with many griefs. But you, man of God, flee from all this, and pursue righteousness, godliness, faith, love, endurance and gentleness 1 Timothy 6:6-11 NIV. (Underlined for emphasis)

Godly riches are always better than worldly riches!

Some radio and television preachers rightly teach certain principles concerning God's word. They fail, however, when they equate godliness with prosperity. Pam and I have learned to sow seed in good soil, but when someone tells me to give $1000.00 and promises I will get $10,000.00, I want to suggest they give His House Church $1,000.00 so they will get a $10,000 return!

Any Scriptural Truth can be preached universally. It will work in India just like it does in America. Here is a sure promise: seek first the Kingdom of God and his righteousness, and He will add all things unto you. There are times godly people lack! Consider some heroes from the hall of faith in Hebrews 11.

> They were stoned; they were sawed in two; they were put to death by the sword. They went about in sheepskins and goatskins, destitute, persecuted and mistreated-the world was not worthy of them. They wandered in

deserts and mountains, and in caves and holes in the ground. Hebrews 11:37-38 NIV. ^(Underlined for emphasis)

Godly people are willing to become poor to make others rich.

The contention between the herdsmen of Lot and Abraham in Genesis 12 illustrate this. They were running out of pasture because of the overabundance of sheep they had. Rather than looking out for himself, Abraham offered Lot the choice of where to move his flocks and herds. Lot looked around with greedy little eyes and claimed the beautiful plains of Sodom. He and his family were destroyed because he coveted after the flesh rather than looking over the land spiritually. Perhaps Canaanite was at work.

Jesus made himself poor in able to make others rich. He wore the crown of thorns which is a Jewish symbol of poverty so we can break the curse of poverty and walk with greater abundance.

📖 You were bought at a price. Therefore honor God with your body. First Corinthians 6:2 NIV.

Canaanite is subtle, it will make us covet until we are trapped.

If we get our riches from the world, we are bound to the world. If we truly believe "God will supply all our needs" we have no worries or anxiety about money. Everything is God's! He gives me 100% and I give him 10%. Sounds like 90% increase to me! Canaanite uses trafficking and trading to hold us down. This spirit wants to hold people, ministries, and governments in poverty.

If finances keep you in bondage, Canaanite may be at work.

Jesus said if we seek first the Kingdom of God and His righteousness, all we need will be added unto us. We either believe that or not! Surprisingly, I learned this lesson, not when things were going well financially, but when I had to learn to trust in God when things were not going well. It began in 2011 when the lead pastor of our church resigned. For a variety of reasons many who had been faithful to the church left. I honestly didn't know if the church would survive the loss of members and income. Some weeks I wasn't paid at all, and my salary over the next few years fell far short of the budget. It was during these years that Jehovah Jireh proved Himself so faithful to us. We made giving to Missions and First Fruits a priority and it was amazing to see how God began to provide in spite of lower attendance and income.

What about faithful stewards, who
continually face financial difficulties?

Canaanite is just one of many things working to bring financial bondage. Many have vows or curses working against them.

a. Vows to secret societies, etc., can bring financial problems.

Vows are behind many ongoing problems. They should be confessed, renounced, and corresponding spirits cast out. We address vows including personal or ancestral vows of Free Masonry in our seminar *Deliverance from Curses, Iniquities, and the Big Five.* Selwyn Stephens has blessed the church world-wide with his prayers of Release from Free Mason prayers available at his website: http://jubileeresources.org/

b. Curses bring financial problems.

The curse of poverty, going all the way back to Adam, is covered in my book *From Woe is Me to Wow is He!*[3] Adam received the curse of poverty when God cursed the ground and said Adam would have thorns and thistles to contend with. The thorn bush became a symbol of poverty for Israel. Jesus, by shedding the blood of his head when He wore a crown of thorns, made it possible for us to break the curse of poverty and invoke His redemption for our prosperity. If you feel your finances are cursed, seek revelation as to their cause, confess personal and ancestral sin, and break them with the blood of Jesus.

The Midianite curse brings financial problems.

When people never seem to be able to break free financially there may be a Midianite curse at work. This is especially true when they experience a yearly cycle of financial difficulties. We will look at that in the next chapter.

Breaking Canaanite Curses and Evicting Canaanite Spirits:

- Father we confess and repent of all personal, ancestral, and corporate greed.
- We confess and repent of all personal or ancestral withholding of tithes and offerings.
- We confess where we and our ancestors have been brought low by unwise business dealing.
- We confess and repent of personal or ancestral coveting and putting things before You, for we cannot serve both God and money.

- We bind the Canaanite Strongman and demolish its stronghold.
- We cast down:
  - Pride.
  - Greed.
  - Covetousness.
  - And every Canaanite spirit.
  - In Jesus' Name, amen. (Expel)
- We also bind the strongman Mammon and Babylon. We demolish their strongholds in our lives and cast them down in the powerful name of Jehovah Jireh, our provider. (Expel)
- We command every foul spirit and principality to take your hands-off God's property. Loose our money, property, job, finances, and possessions, in Jesus' Name.
- Lord Jesus, You are Son, Savior, and our Deliverer.
- You promised to meet all our needs, not only mental and spiritual, but practical as well.
- Therefore, in Your name, I yield to You my possessions and right of ownership.
- I surrender my body, mind, intellect, emotions, and everything I own to the Lord.
- I proclaim the redemption of Christ over all my finances.

Endnotes:

[1]*The Seven Mountain Prophecy* – Johnny Enlow – Summary Sheet
http://www.the7mountains.com/2010/01/24/the-seven-mountain-prophecy-johnny-enlow-summary-sheet/
[2]The New York Times/*Money Fights Predict Divorce Rates.*
http://economix.blogs.nytimes.com/2009/12/07/money-fights-predict-divorce-rates/
[3]*From Woe is Me to Wow is He!* Douglas Carr, Create Space 2016. Doug also has a seminar by the same name which covers the seven places Jesus shed His blood so we can break seven specific curses and redeem seven specific blessings.

7 MIDIANITE

Personal and ancestral curses open portals for demons to kill, steal, and destroy.

Just as oaths and vows give demons license to attack; curses, whether personal or ancestral, give demons legal permission to wage war until the curse is broken, the legal permission is renounced, and the portal is closed to Satan.

Midianite curses must be broken so Midianite spirits can be cast down.

I had a lot of interruptions while I working on this teaching. We had roofers and contractors working on our church who needed time and attention. Our heating contractor was fine-tuning our new boiler system, and he brought many decisions to me. With all this, I felt my work was fragmented and missing something. I went home around 5:00, knowing we had to leave at 5:30 for a revival meeting. While waiting, I quickly checked my email which contained the missing piece: a wonderful testimony from a young wife and mother of four children ranging from two to twelve years old.

We had a very effective deep healing appointment with this mother, but she was having trouble at home, with her finances, with her husband, and was having serious problems with her three-year-old. She shared how her family was hit with strife *every* October. I told her cyclical things, whether seasonal or multiplication of the age things started such as age 7, 14, 21, etc. are often connected to Midianite. I encouraged her to ask God where this curse came into her family and told her how to confess, renounce, and break the curse and resist the spirits. I also encouraged her to go over the prayers breaking the death and dumb spirit from my book *Free Indeed from Root Spirits.*[1]

This mother's testimony was so good I asked permission to share it as we study Midianite:

October 24. Hi! Update - I was led to the Midianite curse - Prayed through that with my hubby - I went through the time and land curse -WOW. My hubby was born on Oct 16, unwanted by both parents. We ALWAYS, attend a "fall Halloween activity" that weekend, we have miscarried in October, lost family members, experienced financial ruin...ALL in October. I can't believe I missed that all this time. I prayed with authority over the spirit of control and deaf and dumb that was suffocating my home, myself, my husband, and my children.

After the prayer, my husband went and cleaned his entire truck (it was FULL of five garbage bags of stuff), I was able to catch up on house work and school, I FINALLY had another prophetic word for myself and a friend going through a crisis, AND money just appeared in our bank account...it was gone and then it came back. I can't even explain it.

She went on to say: My three-year-old has had no seizure activity and my littlest who was terrified of her bedroom has napped in there peacefully two days now! Thank you!! So excited with what God is doing to cleanse our family. This woman's testimony inspires us to deal with Midianite!

Midianite is empowered by curse to victimize you.

Midianite spirits worked through the Midianite tribe to take advantage of Joseph, using his brothers' greed and jealousy. The Midianites were opportunists. They didn't take possession of cities, but attacked to steal the harvest each year. The hand of Midian is seen when Joseph is sold by his own brothers.

📖 Then <u>Midianite traders passed by</u>; so the brothers pulled Joseph up and lifted him out of the pit, and sold him to the Ishmaelites for twenty shekels of silver. And they took Joseph to Egypt. Genesis 37:28 NKJV. _(Underlined for emphasis)

Joseph, overcame his brothers mistreatment of selling him to the Midianite traders and pretending he had been killed by wild beasts. Several years later, Joseph told his brothers how they meant all this for evil, but God used it for good (Genesis 50:20).

Midianite empowers others to take advantage of you.

Consider Moses and Joseph. Moses' father-in-law didn't seem concerned for his son-in-law. He only looked out for himself. Whether the perpetrator or the victim, Midianite seeks to bring people down concerning finances and destiny.

📖 Now Moses said to Hobab the son of Reuel the Midianite, Moses' father-in-law, "We are setting out for the place of which the Lord said, 'I will give it to you.' Come with us, and we will treat you well; for the Lord has promised good things to Israel." And he said to him, "I will not go, but I will depart to my own land and to my relatives." So Moses said, "Please do not leave, inasmuch as you know how we are to camp in the wilderness, and you can be our eyes. And it shall be, if you go with us—indeed it shall be—that whatever good the Lord will do to us, the same we will do to you." Numbers 10:29-31 NKJV. (Underlined for emphasis)

Moses served Reuel faithfully, but like Laban with Joseph, Reuel was quick to take advantage of Moses but hesitant to help him or bless him. He was in it for himself and not for Moses.

Midianite uses personal sin to bring corporate ruin.

📖 And indeed, one of the children of Israel came and presented to his brethren a Midianite woman in the sight of Moses and in the sight of all the congregation of the children of Israel, who were weeping at the door of the tabernacle of meeting. Now when Phinehas the son of Eleazar, the son of Aaron the priest, saw it, he rose from among the congregation and took a javelin in his hand; and he went after the man of Israel into the tent and thrust both of them through, the man of Israel, and the woman through her body. So the plague was stopped among the children of Israel. And those who died in the plague were twenty-four thousand. Numbers 25:6-9 NKJV. (Underlined for emphasis)

If you hit your thumb with a hammer your whole body says ouch. It's a mistake to think personal sin doesn't affect the family, church, or community. The whole nation of Israel suffered because one man gave into Midianite seduction. Pastors and church members take a horrible risk when they overlook personal sin in the congregation. One person's sin can destroy the entire body. Think of key leaders or pastors who sin and how it affects a church. Consider how personal sin of well-known pastors and evangelists have brought reproach upon faith communities.

Midianite must be dealt with.

God didn't tell Moses to just love, accept and forgive the Midianites. He told him to deal with them (Numbers 25:16-17; 31:1-3)! We cannot tolerate sin in the camp and we should not tolerate Midianite in our lives, homes, or churches.

📖 The Lord said to Moses, "Treat the Midianites as enemies and kill them." Numbers 25:16-17 NIV. (Underlined for emphasis)

One of the last things God told Moses to do was take vengeance on the Midianites.

📖 And the Lord spoke to Moses, saying: "Take vengeance on the Midianites for the children of Israel. Afterward you shall be gathered to your people." So Moses spoke to the people, saying, "Arm some of yourselves for war, and let them go against the Midianites to take vengeance for the Lord on Midian. Numbers 31:1-3 NKJV. (Underlined for emphasis)

God may use Midianite spirits to discipline wayward people.

God disciplines those He loves (Hebrews 12:5-11). I personally attest His discipline will be as severe as needed to bring correction. God is sovereign. Scripture shows how God hardened Pharaoh's heart (Exodus 9:12) and how an evil spirit sent from the Lord tormented Saul (1 Samuel 16:14). God **gave** the Israelites into the hands of the Midianites. Judges gives one notable example.

📖 The Israelites did evil in the eyes of the Lord, and for seven years he gave them into the hands of the Midianites. Because the power of Midian was so oppressive, the Israelites prepared shelters for themselves in mountain clefts, caves and strongholds. Judges 6:1-2 NIV. (Underlined for emphasis)

Midianite seeks to plunder the harvest.

The Midianites were squatters who pillaged the land. Consider how the Midianites stole the harvest from Israel each year.

📖 Whenever the Israelites planted their crops, the Midianites, Amalekites and other eastern peoples invaded the country. They camped on the land and ruined the crops all the way to Gaza and did not spare a living thing for Israel, neither sheep nor cattle nor donkeys. They came up with their livestock and their tents like swarms of locusts. It was impossible to count them or their camels; they invaded the land to ravage it. Midian so impoverished the Israelites that they cried out to the Lord for help. Judges 6:3-6 NIV. (Underlined for emphasis)

As a young man, I tried to save up enough money to buy shingles for the roof of my first house. Every time I had nearly enough saved up, I had an unexpected expense like a doctor bill, car repair, utility increase or something that robbed my savings. That is how Midianite works.

Sadly, many people and nations must come to a point of desperation before they start calling out to the Lord. Our city officials called me to lead a prayer meeting for the city the week after the Twin Towers were destroyed by Terrorists. People realize they need God when tragedy happens. Unfortunately, that desperation seems to slip away when people feel safe again.

There is a cry God hears:

A mother can hear her child's cry of desperation even over the sounds of other children running, playing and screaming. God always hears a cry of desperation. The Israelites finally came to such desperation they began crying out to the Lord.

a. God's response to them was sending a prophetic word!

They were given another chance to hear and respond to the Lord's Word (Judges 6:7-10). God will test people, if they pass the test He blesses them. When they fail the test, he gives them another test. God tested the Israelites repeatedly concerning whether they would give in or resist Midianite temptation and attacks.

📖 When the Israelites cried out to the Lord because of Midian, <u>he sent them a prophet,</u> who said, "This is what the Lord, the God of Israel, says: I brought you up out of Egypt, out of the land of slavery. I rescued you from the hand of the Egyptians. And I delivered you from the hand of all your oppressors; I drove them out before you and gave you their land. I said to you, 'I am the Lord your God; do not worship the gods of the Amorites, in whose land you live.' <u>But you have not listened to me.</u>" Judges 6:7-10 NIV. ^(Underlined for emphasis)

b. God's second response to their cry was to call a man for the task.

God will not be a pawn in man's hand. Nor will He call people to be pawns in His hands! God usually raises up a man or a woman in answer to our prayers.

📖 The angel of the Lord came and sat down under the oak in Ophrah that belonged to Joash the Abiezrite, where his son Gideon was threshing wheat in a winepress <u>to keep it from the Midianites.</u> When the angel of the Lord appeared to Gideon, he said, "The Lord is with you, mighty warrior." Judges 6:11-12 NIV. (Underlined for emphasis)

c. God's calling is God's enabling.

I lacked confidence when I was called to preach. My first wife accurately summed it up when I was offered a church, "you don't know how to preach." I was afraid of public speaking, and my vocational analysis test in college said I was best suited to be a funeral director. I shared my fears and frustrations with my psychology professor and he wrote on my paper "God's calling is God's enabling." I, like Gideon, needed to learn that truth.

📖 "Pardon me, my lord," Gideon replied, "but if the Lord is with us, <u>why has all this happened to us?</u> Where are all his wonders that our ancestors told us about when they said, 'Did not the Lord bring us up out of Egypt?' But now the Lord has abandoned us and given us into the hand of Midian." The Lord turned to him and said, "Go in the strength you have and save Israel out of Midian's hand. Am I not sending you?" "Pardon me, my lord," Gideon replied, "<u>but how can I save Israel? My clan is the weakest in Manasseh, and I am the least in my family." Judges 6:13-15 NIV. (Underlined for emphasis)

God delights in using unqualified people to display His glory.

📖 The Lord answered, "I will be with you, and you will strike down all the Midianites, leaving none alive." Gideon replied, "If now I have found favor in your eyes, give me a sign that it is really you talking to me. Please do not go away until I come back and bring my offering and set it before you." And the Lord said, "I will wait until you return." Judges 6:16-18 NIV. (Underlined for emphasis)

The story of how God used Gideon and a reduced army of 300 to defeat the Midianites is found in Judges Chapter Seven. Unfortunately, Midianite tried to sneak in from other directions. First the men of Ephraim had a pity party because Gideon didn't call them to the battle (Judges 8:1-3).

Even the spoil from Midian left a gap in Gideon's armor.

After Gideon's conquering of the Midianites, he was tempted to pride, especially after the Israelites asked him to rule over them. Gideon asked for the spoil of gold earrings from the plunder and used them make the gold into an ephod which he placed in Ophrah, his home town.

There is good reason God warns His people not to touch things that have been dedicated or sacrificed to demons. The spoil from the Midianites led to Gideon's downfall.

📖 Gideon made the gold into an ephod, which he placed in Ophrah, his town. All Israel prostituted themselves by worshiping it there, and it became a snare to Gideon and his family. Judges 8:27 NIV. (Underlined for emphasis)

There is much more we learn about the Midianite curse. You may want to study further how the Midianites brought a curse against Israel's prosperity and promise. If you do so, try to find what Israel did or did not do that brought them under such a curse, and I would love to have you share with me what you learn.

Open doors to Midianite:

a. Putting comfort and security before stewardship to God, family, church or the larger community.

When people put meals out, recreation, careless spending and the like before being responsible to God and for family and the Lord's, work, Midianite has an open door. Midianite is a devourer that takes advantage of people who do not tithe and properly care for their families.

b. Trying to be "Jehovah Jireh" by thinking "I can provide everything I am my family need to possess our birthright."

Jehovah is our provider. Midianite slips in when we consider self as soul provider. Pride stands behind "I can do it all myself, I don't need God." I think of a friend whose father who refused to join in saying grace before a meal. He said, "I earned this food with my own hands – God didn't give it to me and I won't thank him for it."

c. Thinking "It is mine, Mine, MINE, and I can do whatever I want with it.

If you are old enough, you might call this the "Daffy Duck" anointing. If you or someone in your generational line treated material things as their own, with no respect to how God wanted them to steward their property and possessions, Midianite is at work.

The Midianite curse is suspect when:

a. You are unable to obtain enough assets or wealth to leverage change.

Some people never get ahead, regardless of how much they earn. They buy new vehicles before they finish paying for their older ones. They constantly pay late fees, and if a special need comes up, they always have to borrow to meet the need. Midianite may be involved.

b. Things like health, finances, and relationships break in a seasonal manner.

When people have yearly cycles of crisis, it may be the work of a Midianite. I wish I had known this when I went through a 7-year cycle of trauma that hit every Father's Day weekend. It started because my personal issues with my father were not addressed. Many of them carried over to my first marriage because I did not address them with a right spirit. Then my first wife left me to rear three children on Father's Day weekend, 1987. I soon left the ministry, thinking God could never use me again since I failed in marriage. On Father's Day weekend 1988, I was depressed to the point of wishing to die. I knew I needed to live for my children's sake so I sold all my guns, gritted my teeth and carried on. On Father's Day weekend 1989, I was thrown off a horse and dragged down a paved road. That caused closed head injury and a $2,700.00 deductible to be flown by helicopter to a trauma unit. On Father's Day weekend 1990, I reached my lowest point spiritually. Around that same time in 1991, we had a house fire.

Things began turning for me around on Father's Day weekend 1992 when Pastor Jack Eitelbuss invited me to preach at his church. Somehow that broke the curse and redirected my path.

c. You lack freedom to accumulate resources year after year so you fall further behind financially rather than getting ahead.

Other manifestations of a Midianite curse include: poverty, devouring, stealing, fear, hiding, slavery, trauma, death, deprived, feeling unprotected, comfortless, hope deferred, abuse, manipulation/control, or wrong use of finances. Additional characteristics of being under a Midianite curse include: selfishness, self-centeredness, strife, deception, freed, rebellion, pride, idolatry, and occult.

The Midianite Curse often called "the giver's curse."

Arthur Burk told how his family went through financial crisis every May for years. They tithed, were generous with offerings, first-fruits, supporting missionaries, sowing good seed, etc. Even though they followed God's standards in giving, they still had financial crisis every May until they received ministry from a woman who broke the Midianite curse and delivered them. The following May and since they have received financial blessings every May.

Paul tells us that the things that happened to the Israelites in the Old Testament are examples to keep us from setting our hearts on the evil things they did (1 Corinthians 10:6). Each ungodly nation is an example of curse and foul spirit we need to defeat. Some people have continuing battles with fear, confusion, and contention even after they are saved. The word Midianite means confusion, fear and contention. God is a God of peace and order, and something is always wrong when the people of God are full of fear, confusion, and contention.

Signs of confusion coming from Midianite:

a.   Confusion from a mixture of truth & error in thinking.

If I am guilty--woe to me! Even if I am innocent, I cannot lift my head, for I am full of shame and drowned in my affliction. Job 10:15 NIV. (Underlined for emphasis)

Job was confused as to why a righteous man should suffer. We are mistaken if we think bad things never happen to good people. Some teach if you have faith, you always have perfect health, peace, and prosperity. Job couldn't understand why he lost everything. After all, he was trying to live a godly life.

b. Contention from not recognizing God in a situation.

God used conflict *and* contention to defeat the Midianite camp. The Midianites were stronger than Gideon's army. But when Gideon and his men smashed some jars and sounded some trumpets, the Midianites became so confused they started attacking each other rather than their enemy (Judges 7:22).

How often does that happen in marriages when financial troubles hit? Rather than coming to the Lord together to work out a solution, husbands and wives start blaming each other, often to the point it leads to separation or divorce which can cost thousands of dollars more than working together to solve problems.

Couples don't have put up with continual conflict. They don't need to keep on fighting each other rather than the enemy! When we cast off confusion and contention, we grow through difficult situations rather than running from them. God allows us to face problems so we will learn to look up and grow up. God wants to use problems in a home or church to lead us to seek growth in Him. The devil wants to use them to bring us down.

We must to learn to attack problems rather than people:

a. Confusion from not making God first in life and family.

📖 Again the Israelites did evil in the eyes of the LORD, and for <u>seven years</u> he gave them into the hands of the Midianites. Judges 6:1.
<small>(Underlined for emphasis)</small>

Too many Believers receive Jesus as savior, but do not follow Him as Lord. It is when we confess Him as Lord (Master, Boss, Supreme Ruler) of our lives that we are delivered from evil and given great authority over powers of darkness. The Israelites repeatedly chose to please themselves rather than God. God, therefore, repeatedly handed them over to their enemy.

The same thing happens to us. In *Choosing Kingdom*[2] I share: we all choose continually between the Kingdom of God or the kingdom of self. Every choice, every circumstance calls us to make that choice. When we follow Jesus as Lord, we choose to seek first the Kingdom of God and His righteousness. When we don't submit completely to Jesus as Lord, we choose the kingdom of self and its consequences.

b. Confusion from blaming God for *our* mistakes. (Judges 6:7-10)

Henry Youngman jokingly said "A good wife forgives her husband when SHE is wrong." In similar fashion, Israel blamed God for problems of their own making. God declared "you didn't obey me." Midianite questions why God does bad things to us. Holy Spirit moves us to ask revelation what we and our ancestors have done to bring evil upon us.

c. Confusion of thinking God is powerless or doesn't care.

Midianite will do whatever possible to make people think God is unloving. It tempts us to think either God doesn't care, God isn't there, God is angry, or God isn't big enough to solve our problems. Just like Gideon, we wonder why has all this happened to us if the LORD is with us? We echo Gideon every time we face problems saying, "God, why have You gotten me into this mess - why aren't You doing something about it?"

e. Confusion from thinking God will fix it without you.

The LORD told Gideon to "Go in the strength you have and save Israel out of Midian's hand. Am I not sending you?" Gideon thought "I am the runt, of a runt family, of a runt tribe, of a runt nation, and God will have to find somebody else to make things better." "Here I am, God, use somebody else" (Judges 6:14-18).

How often do we get it mixed up, telling God how to fix things, rather than asking Him how He wants us to fix them? Do you see the difference? God wanted to save the Israelites, but he wanted to use Gideon to do it. Gideon wanted God to "fix things," without his having get out of the wine vat. God says, "We're in this together and I want to use you, buddy."

The Midianite Spirit Works Where There is Confusion. Confusion is a mixture of faith and doubt, error and truth, obedience and rebellion. Consider the Story of Manasseh. Gideon was of the half tribe of Manasseh. Half the tribe stayed on the other side of the Jordan and Gideon's side came in.

We must pull down wrong order so Divine order can be established.

Midianite works in difficult seasons.

We first see Gideon hiding in a wine vat for fear of what the Midianite raiders were going to do. During difficult seasons, families either pull together or fall apart.

God uses problems to unify; Satan uses them to divide.

People who lose a child or have special needs children either pull together, or fall apart. They are far more likely to divorce than parents of "normal" or healthy children unless they come together in the Lord. Families facing serious illness or financial problems are more likely to break up unless they face their problems together. Fear, confusion, and contention come during difficult times. God can refine us through them, if we resist His grace, the devil uses them destroy.

Problems make us better or bitter.

Romans 8:28 basically tells us that God will not waste any problem when people are called, submitted, and pray over their problems in the Spirit. If, however, people fail to look to the Lord in seasons of trial, they are likely to become bitter.

Midianite works where there is pain.

Job couldn't understand why the righteous had to suffer. To make matters worse, his miserable, accusing friends show up and say "none of these things happen to a righteous man." Job was confused because there was a mixture of truth and error in thinking. Job's testing turned into a testimony however. Even when Satan tried to destroy him, Job did not curse God with his lips. He kept the integrity of his confession.

Midianite works in times of defeat.

David's life shows how shame and defeat can bring confusion.

📖 My disgrace is before me all day long, and my face is covered with shame at the taunts of those who reproach and revile me, because of the enemy, who is bent on revenge. Psalm 44:15-16 NIV.

Christians shoot themselves and their own wounded. Rather than crying out to God, they condemn themselves and others. That is the devil's job. Our job is to forgive and intercede!

Midianite works in times of disorder.

📖 For God is not a God of disorder but of peace. 1 Cor. 14:33a.

Confusion moves among people when things are not done decently and in order. While freedom in the Spirit is great, if there is no biblical leadership structure, everyone becomes wise in their own eyes, confusion sets in, and the bond of peace is broken.

That is why God gives instructions of how many are supposed to prophecy, or speak in tongues in public meetings (1 Corinthians 14:26-32). It is error to think God blesses lack of preparation! There are times that the Holy Spirit leads us beyond what we have prepared for, but as we seek Him, He also leads our preparation.

Midianite works when we lack direction.

Think how frustrating it is to climb into a car with friends and no one can decide what restaurant they want to go to. When everybody says "I don't care," it becomes even more confusing until someone finally offers direction. God established apostolic five-fold leadership because He knows how badly we need direction.

Midianite works when everybody wants their own way.

Whether choosing a place to eat, what program to watch, or what to do on a day off, strife and disorder comes in when everybody wants to do their own thing. That is why some church building or remodeling plans result in splits. The only way to avoid such is to seek the good of the group rather than personal desire. James clarifies this:

📖 Who is wise and understanding among you? Let them show it by their good life, by deeds done in the humility that comes from wisdom. <u>But if you harbor bitter envy and selfish ambition in your hearts,</u> do not boast about it or deny the truth. Such "<u>wisdom</u>" does not come down from heaven but <u>is earthly, unspiritual, demonic.</u> For where you have envy and selfish ambition, there you find disorder and every evil practice. James 3:13-16. (Underlined for emphasis)

There are several prayers given to break Midianite curses and cast out Midianite spirits. I integrated a few in a simple prayer of confessing, repenting, renouncing, breaking, and casting off. At the end of this section I include references which contain prayers concerning Midianite from Arthur Burk[3] and the King's Court.[4]

BREAKING MIDIANITE CURSES/SPIRITS:

- In Jesus' Name, we bind the Midianite strongman and demolish Midianite strongholds.
- Heavenly Father, we confess and repent of all personal and ancestral faithlessness that has kept us and our families from possessing our birthright.
- We confess and repent of personal and ancestral falling out of Your order and Your timing or seasons for our lives.
- We confess and repent of all personal and ancestral wrong gain, selfishness, stealing, lying, or withholding of blessings from others.
- We ask you to cleanse us and our generational lines of such iniquities.
- In Jesus' Name, we ask You to break the power of every Midianite curse in us and our family line.
- We confess our dependence upon You, Lord.
- We decree You will supply all our needs according to Your riches in Christ Jesus.

✝ Father, we ask You to break every stronghold of Midianite and bring us into the place of Your blessings per Your plan and seasons for our lives.

✝ Now in the Name and through the blood of the Lord Jesus Christ, we break every Midianite curse and command Midianite spirits and the Midianite strongman to loose us and go Now! (Expel)

✝ Holy Spirit, lead us into the fullness of Jehovah's plan for our times and seasons.

✝ In Jesus' Name, Amen.

Endnotes:

[1]*Free Indeed from Root Spirits.* Doug Carr, Create Space. 2014

[2]*Choosing Kingdom.* Doug Carr, Create Space. Hopefully 2016.

Further prayers for Midianite:

[3]Arthur Burk:

http://www.freebibledownload.net/7BiblicalCursesAndDeliveranceP rayers/TheSevenBiblicalCursesDeliverancePrayers.pdf

[4]PRAYER FOR BREAKING THE CURSE OF POVERTY:

https://www.google.com/url?sa=t&rct=j&q=&esrc=s&source=web &cd=1&cad=rja&uact=8&ved=0ahUKEwi71tmT5svQAhXnwlQK HT_MAEIQFggtMAA&url=http%3A%2F%2Fthekingscourtcalabar .blogspot.com%2F2013%2F04%2Fprayer-points-for-midianite-curses.html&usg=AFQjCNFsjZn_cGnj8LKmRuqabjA7FJ5wmQ&si g2=MGLcDlCyWHctjnitX3XVVQ

8 GIRGASHITE

I summarize Johnny Enlow's summary of the Girgashite assignment as follows: It works on the Mountain of Government. Girgashites (represent corruption) are the Enemy of this mountain. They work under the principality Lucifer (pride and manipulation) to displace the significant authority of Apostles to fill government with positions with humble, servant leaders with integrity, to bring the Revelation 5:12 Key: Power.[1]

The Girgashite role is to stir and raise up whatever would prevent or hinder God's prophetic destiny over nations and individuals.

Girgashite literally means "dwelling on clayey soil." The wise man builds his house on the rock – not on clay. Individuals and nations fulfill their redemptive purpose when on Christ the solid rock they stand. I was hiking in Lost Nations Park when it started to rain. When I returned to the car, it couldn't get traction on the slick clay road. We walked several miles to borrow a tractor, and even the tractor couldn't move the car until I drove off the drive an onto the sod. Clay represents being on slippery clay where you can't move forward.

Girgashite is a pig like.

Shama Elim wrote an article "The Girgashite pigs"[2] that challenged my thinking. I took a few thoughts from it and share them, in my own words.

The passage about the demonized Gadarene in Matthew 8 refers to the Girgashite people of Deuteronomy 7:1. Pig herding was an important local industry in the territory of the Gadarenes. Pigs, as we all know, love to roll around in the mud, so they are a perfect representation of the Girgashite spirit, since "Girgashite" means "clay dweller." Girgashites are constantly focused on earthly things, the same way pigs are always looking towards the ground to find something to eat. The writer says "I have heard that it is physically impossible for pigs to look up at the sky (I have never asked a pig if this is true, but it sounds true to me); this makes sense since the Girgashite spirit leads people away from focusing on heavenly things, on things of eternal nature, on the things above." [Ibid3] Later the writer says:

> Much like the pigs, Girgashite people are "violent runners." Since they rarely take the time to ask God what He wants, they usually make impulsive decisions based on a short-sighted vision that is completely focused on the ground. Girgashites make decisions the way a bull charges towards the bullfighter's cape. [Ibid]

Jesus cast the legion of demons into the pigs who ran over the cliff and drowned (see Mark 5). This was in the region of Gerasenes where pagans ate pork and sacrificed pigs to their false gods. As pigs return to their mudholes, Girgashite returns to sin. Pigs are built to look down, root around, and get fat. They can't look up at the stars. If you are praying for someone who eats like a pig, or stinks like a pig, or can't look up, or keeps returning to his or her old mudholes - you may want to check for Girgashite!

Girgashite is a curse and spirit of backsliding.

📖 As a dog returns to his own vomit, So a fool repeats his folly. Proverbs 22:11 NKJV.

I know a pastor who runs a treatment center for addicts. He sends some for deliverance. Many are under a Girgashite curse with Girgashite spirits always trying to lead them back into the destruction of previous sin. Why do people, who have tasted the goodness of God return to behaviors which destroy them and their families? It may be Girgashite!

Girgashite takes people back to the filth God saved them from.

I quote from the article *Destroying the "Girgashite Giant,"* by "In Jesus."

The "Girgashite giant" or spirit is the spirit of backsliding.

This spirit will team up with any other wicked spirit to get you, of your own free will and decision, to give up and turn back to the world, the flesh, and to Satan. The word "Girgashite" has two meanings. One meaning is "one who turns back from a pilgrimage" and the second meaning is "dweller in clay soil or black mud." This giant seeks to turn us back from obeying and following Christ Jesus, and to become earthly and sensually evil again. This evil spirit is one of Satan's most powerful spirits. This evil spirit pursues us and persuades us to turn from our eternal inheritance, back to the blackness and filth of Egypt from which we have fled. The "Girgashite giant" is the spirit that causes the greatest temptations of our past against us. This spirit specializes in reminding us of past sexual pleasures, past feelings involving drugs, liquor, etc. This spirit works hard using our thoughts, feelings and emotions to dwell and to live in our past lives and memories.

Scriptural examples of the "Girgashite spirit" destroying the hearts of God's people to cause them to cancel their salvation. Notice carefully in these references, this giant uses their lust, their fears and doubts, causes trouble, and keeps the hearts and mind on the past.[3]

Girgashite draws us back to Egypt.

Egypt is a biblical picture of the world. The children of Israel wanted to head back to their leeks, cucumbers and garlic, even if that meant return to slavery. Believers are brought out of the world and into the ecclesia - the Church -- The Called-Out Ones. We are called out of the world and into God's Kingdom so we can be a blessing to this world.

📖 But *ye* [are] a chosen race, a <u>kingly priesthood</u>, a holy nation, a people for a possession, that ye might set forth the excellencies of him who has called you out of darkness to his wonderful light. 1 Peter 2:9-12 DBY. (Underlined for emphasis)

We are to set on minds our things above and not things below. Jesus commands us to deny ourselves, take up our cross, and follow him! The Israelites had to learn they lived not by bread alone, but by every word which proceeds from the mouth of God. We need to set our minds on things above – the unseen things which are eternal, rather than the things we can taste, touch, feel, smell, and see. It is the lust of the eyes and the lust of the flesh which drives people back into the world.

Girgashite brings compromise.

People under a Girgashite curse battle by degree. They compromise a little, then a little more. Their focus slips away from spiritual things and falls back, bit by bit, to soulish activities. It deadens the conscience to where little sins don't seem bad anymore. They start with one thought, taste, or touch and it leads them back into bondage.

The doctrine of grace has been perverted and many believe they can go on sinning because Jesus died for their sins past, present and future. The true message of grace recognizes that Jesus gives us the desire and power to do His will, depart from sin, and live in victory.

An example of how we are to leave the world of darkness and walk in the kingdom of light is given in Judges Six as false altars were pulled down and the second bull was to be sacrificed. The second bull (which means servant) was seven years old (which is the number of perfection). It represented the perfect Christ who is the perfect sacrifice and came not to be served but to serve.

That same night the Lord said to him, "Take the second bull from your father's herd, the one seven years old. <u>Tear down your father's altar to Baal and cut down the Asherah pole beside it</u>. Judges 6:25 NIV. ^(Underlined for emphasis)

Things that stood in the place of God were cut off.

Girgashite lures people to hang onto things which distance them from God. They allow the grip of pornography, materialism, addictions, and sinful relationships stand between them and the Lord. Through Christ we must cut such things off!

The picture of sacrificing our lives as perfect servants was given.

We are to give our bodies in sacrifice to God even as Jesus did.

I beseech you therefore, brethren, by the mercies of God, that you <u>present your bodies a living sacrifice</u>, <u>holy</u>, <u>acceptable to God</u>, which is your reasonable service. Romans 12:1 NKJV. (Underlined for emphasis)

Jesus didn't go to the cross so we wouldn't have to. He went to the cross so we could become living sacrifices, take up our personal cross, and follow Him all the way! Girgashite doesn't like that idea, but Jesus does.

📖 Then Jesus said to His disciples, "If anyone desires to come after Me, <u>let him deny himself</u>, and <u>take up his cross</u>, and <u>follow Me</u>. For whoever desires to save his life will lose it, but whoever loses his life for My sake will find it. For what profit is it to a man if he gains the whole world, and loses his own soul? Or what will a man give in exchange for his soul? Matt. 16:24-27. NKJV. (Underlined for emphasis)

Girgashite brings chaos.

Chaos is the absence of Divine order. Worldly systems must be cast down so God's order can arise. Even churches need to shake off worldly systems, because so many are built on worldly foundations. The Church is to be laid on the foundation of Christ.

If we are founded on Jesus Christ, we can cast down worldly church government, and build on the divine structure of apostles, prophets, evangelists, pastors, and teachers. Christian leadership is accountable to God, to the fivefold ministry, and to the congregation. Any pastor or person who thinks he/she is accountable only to God will be led into error like Balaam who was not accountable to "anyone but God."

Girgashite causes apostasy.

Second Thessalonians 2:3 says the man of sin shall not be revealed until there will be apostasy or falling away. To know the Lord Jesus Christ and love him then fall away is apostasy.

📖 Let no one deceive you by any means; for that Day will not come unless <u>the falling away comes first</u>, and the man of sin is revealed, the son of perdition. 2 Thessalonians 2:3 NKJV. (Underlined for emphasis)

Paul sadly reported how his friend Demas fell into apostasy.

📖 For Demas, <u>because he loved this world</u>, has deserted me and has gone to Thessalonica. 2 Timothy 4:10a NIV. ^(Underlined for emphasis)

This is what Jesus meant about putting the hand to the plow and turning back. If you don't keep your eye on what's ahead, your path will veer from the straight and narrow way.

📖 But Jesus said to him, "No one, having put his hand to the plow, and looking back, <u>is fit for the kingdom of God</u>." Luke 9:62 NKJV. ^(Underlined for emphasis)

Girgashite causes one to turn back to the pleasures of this world.

Jesus gave this warning before pornography was available on computer. He warned about it before so many people were broken that it became easy to find a one-night stand. He warned about it before drugs became so rampant. He warned how such things can make our love grow cold. He says "Stand firm to the end!"

📖 Because of the increase of wickedness, the love of most will grow cold, but he who stands firm to the end will be saved. Matt. 24:12-13 NIV.

People often pray and have spiritual breakthrough. But then, instead of standing firm, they relax, step back a little, and lose all they've gained. They stop reading the Bible and praying. They soon drop out of church and fall away from the Lord.

The world is always trying to pull us away from God. We need to resist! The moment we quit resisting the pull of the world, apostasy begins. That is why Paul warned us:

📖 <u>Examine yourselves as to whether you are in the faith</u>. Test yourselves. Do you not know yourselves, that Jesus Christ is in you? —unless indeed you are disqualified. 2 Cor. 13:5 NKJV.
(Underlined for emphasis)

Girgashite tries to make us break away.

People have left the church in droves over the past fifteen years. The Church is still Christ's Body, and He is still the head. If we are disconnected from the Body, we are disconnected from the Head! We must be consistent and persistent. We must keep that which we have committed. We can't step out of line with God and expect him to bless.

Girgashite schemes to make us disheartened and discouraged.

It throws obstacles in the way to make us give up. "What's the use, I give up, what reason do I have to go on living?" Resist such thinking. Jesus said keep on asking, keep on seeking, keep on knocking. It was by persistence of the widow the judge gave her bread in the middle of the night. By persistency we will win. We must be strong. God gave a stern warning through Jeremiah, even to the point of saying the people needed to return to the preacher, rather than the preacher chasing down the backslider.

📖 Therefore this is what the Lord says: "<u>If you repent, I will restore you that you may serve me</u>; if you utter worthy, not worthless, words, you will be my spokesman. <u>Let this people turn to you</u>, but <u>you must not turn to them</u>. Jeremiah 15:19 NIV. ^(Underlined for emphasis)

Girgashite schemes to make us lose hope.

Loss of hope is distrust of God. When we lose hope, we have quit trusting the Lord. If we believe we are in a hopeless situation, we don't believe God can do anything about it situation any longer. The devil knows if we pray and believe, and don't doubt, we will have what we ask for.

Girgashite schemes to make us look back and lose our place.

Jesus told us to remember Lot's wife! She looked back, perhaps for family, friends, house, or the way things used to be. She lost her place and missed her destiny! Girgashite tempts Christians to look back to things like keeping their tithe for pleasure or their Sundays free to sleep in and play. Such thinking makes us lose our place.

Girgashite schemes to make us grumble and give up.

📖 Jesus declared He is the bread of life and if we come to Him we will never go hungry or thirsty. The Jews, however, started to grumble, saying Jesus' teaching was hard. Even his disciples were grumbling! On hearing it, many of his disciples said, "This is a hard teaching. Who can accept it?" Aware that <u>his disciples were grumbling about this,</u> Jesus said to them, "Does this offend you? Then what if you see the Son of Man ascend to where he was before! <u>The Spirit gives life; the flesh counts for nothing</u>. The words I have spoken to you—they are full of the Spirit and life. John 6:60-63 NIV. ^(Underlined for emphasis)

Grumbling leads to defeat because it focuses on the problem and overlooks the love and power of God Almighty.

Girgashite schemes to make us prayer-less and weak.
Think of how the disciples betrayed Jesus after they failed to stay awake and in the garden before Jesus was arrested. Peter was convinced nothing could make him deny Jesus, but he failed to pray.

Girgashite schemes to make us think failure is final.
Peter didn't think he could ever fail before Jesus was arrested. After he failed, however, he never thought he could succeed again. Fear that failure is final makes people go back to their own ways, just as Peter went back to his boats. Thankfully, Jesus restored Peter and wants to restore each one who has lost his or her way.

The way to defeat the Girgashite spirit is to examine yourself to see if you are standing in the faith. Examine your first love. Look and see if you are still growing and moving forward. To examine and see if we are still doing the first works. If not, it is time to repent before apostasy comes.

Breaking off Girgashite curses/spirits:
- Father, we confess and repent of anywhere we and our ancestors have trusted human government rather than the Kingdom of heaven.
- We confess and repent of any place we have been lured into entitlement thinking.
- We confess and repent of building our homes on sand rather than the Rock.
- We confess and repent of all personal and ancestral pride.
- We confess and repent of all personal and ancestral backsliding or falling away.
- We confess and repent of all personal and ancestral compromise.

- We confess and repent of all personal and ancestral giving into selfishness or chaos.
- We confess and repent of all personal and ancestral apostasy or turning back to the pleasures of this world.
- We confess and repent of all personal and ancestral giving into discouragement, losing hope, or losing our place.
- We confess and repent of all personal and ancestral grumbling, prayerlessness, and thinking failure is final.
- In Jesus Name, we break every Girgashite curse and bind the Girgashite strongman.
- We demolish Girgashite strongholds in Jesus' Mighty Name.
- We cast down: Spirits of pride, manipulation and control, and every Girgashite spirit. Go now, in Jesus' Name. (Expel)
- Lord Jesus, we ask you to cast down the Girgashite strongman from our lives, families, and ministries.
- We declare we will seek first the Kingdom of God and forcibly advance it!
- We declare holy alignment of civil laws to God's law.
- We pray officials will tremble at God's Word and walk in fear of the Lord.
- We release a spirit of justice in the land as the armies of heaven restrain evil.
- We pray political leaders will guide with wisdom, revelation, and truth.
- We pray the Supreme Court will reflect the Court of Heaven and the constitution.

Endnotes:

[1]The Seven Mountain Prophecy – Johnny Enlow – Summary Sheet
http://www.the7mountains.com/2010/01/24/the-seven-mountain-prophecy-johnny-enlow-summary-sheet/
[2]The Girgashite pigs http://shamah-elim.info/girgash.htm
[3]http://injesus.com/message-archives/prophetic/Frontlines/girgashite-spirit-going-back-to-the-filth-god-saved

Additional Resources:

[1]See article by Johnny Enlow: Girgashites and the Mountain of Government.
http://www.7culturalmountains.org/apps/articles/default.asp?article id=39113&columnid=4336.
[2]See article on Girgashites and cancer from Shamah Elim.
http://shamah-elim.info/qa/q_cancer.htm

9 HIVITE

Johnny Enlow Summarizes the seven Canaanite spirits and their focused attack on the Seven Mountains of influence as follows. Hivites (represent compromise) are the Enemy of the Mountain of Celebration which includes arts and entertainment. They work under the principality Jezebel (seduction) to displace the significant authority of prophets who have the basic mission to model the greater creative arts of God and prophesy through them. Revelation 5:12 Key: Glory. (Thoughts taken from Enlow's Summary Sheet.)[1]

There were two tribes of Hivites who were both Canaanite. One tribe of the mountains of Lebanon; and the other tribe of the four cities including Gibeon (Judges 3:3). They were descendants of the sixth son of Canaan. "Hivite" speaks of "Delusion or Delight." This word means dweller in a village. The root word means life-giving. Therefore, the word <u>Hivite means a life style or a life that is lived out in the context of a community or a village.</u> It speaks about our relationship with the world.

Proverbs 14:12 is a key verse that every parent should help every child meditate on. Consider both the NKJV and The Message Bible:

📖 There is a way that seems right to a man, But its end is the way of death. Proverbs 14:12 KKJV.

📖 There's a way of life that looks harmless enough; look again—it leads Straight to hell. Sure, those people appear to be having a good time, but all that laughter will end in heartbreak. Proverbs 14:12-13 MSG.

Hivite lures us to participate in things bringing spiritual death. It deals with our association with the world.

Gibeon is a good example of how Hivite works, as we will soon see. Let me ask a question: "Are you as concerned as I am for millennials, college, and career-aged people and their children?"

The devil is far more fastidious in using deceptive means to draw us into worldliness than we realize. We must avoid such deception. If people understood the deception of abortion, they would stand against it. If they understood how Satan is using gaming, cartoons, and television to trap children and adults, they would be careful about what they allow into their homes. We have a choice: sin unto death, or obedience to Jesus unto life (Romans 6:23).

Hivite lures us to believe and live the lie.

Sermon Central speaks of Hivite, saying:

Deception: To mislead by giving a distorted impression or false sense of reality. To trick; to cheat; to beguile. The ancient Greeks used the word to describe the pleasure that comes from watching the theater. Deception is being pacified and placated by unreality. Pain and confusion result from trusting false promises or believing a lie.[2]

Some Hivite style deceptions:
- You only go around once in life, so grab all the gusto you can.
- You deserve a break today . . . (My parents seldom went out to eat. I remember a few visits to the A & W Root Beer stands. That was a huge treat every couple of years.)
- It doesn't matter what you believe, as long as you are sincere.
- There are many roads to heaven which all lead to the same place.

I take the following and highlight the main lies from The Andrew Discipleship School – Kampala MARCH 5, 2014 BY ACHINTORE The Hivite spirit.[3]
- **Know yourself. Socrates.** Study the science of the body and mind.
- **Control yourself. The Stoics.** Self-control. Do good deeds and stop doing bad ones. This will make you better off and good behaviour will save your soul. Obey your conscience and lead a good disciplined life.
- **Adjust yourself. Confucius.** Adapt to the surroundings and follow the trends of society to fit in to society.

✦ **Assert yourself. Nietyche**. Be positive and aggressive. "Drive your own life like a car. You are the centre of your universe. Do not let anyone force you into a mould but break free. Be an individual. It is your life and you should do with it what you like. Why should you conform?"

✦ **Express yourself. Psychologists and Rousseau**. "You are free to do as you like. Cast off traditions and be a unique person in your own right. There are too many "Don'ts." Do your own thing."

✦ **Enjoy yourself. Epicureans.** Eat drink and be merry for tomorrow you may die. Happiness is the most important thing in life. Have no concern beyond the grave. J.S. Mill (concludes) the greatest happiness for the greatest number.

✦ **Suppress yourself. Buddha**. "By suppressing desire, you may end suffering. Follow an eight-fold path to purity. Obey your conscience in right thoughts, right speech, right livelihood, right effort, right mindfulness and right concentration."[3]

How different these lies are from the truth of Jesus who said "If you want to save your life, deny yourself, take up your cross and follow Him." Andrew Discipleship School also shared the strategy of Satan, taking it from how he deceived Adam and Eve in Genesis Three.

The strategy of deception:
> ➢ Distort what God says by changing the emphasis.
> ➢ Bring into question God's motive (always the result of twisted meaning).
> ➢ Introduce reason that ultimately leads you to question God's goodness and integrity.
> ➢ .... Once that's accomplished it's easy to turn you against God's authority.[4]

The Hivite spirit makes us prone to deception:
Joshua 9:3-19 illustrates how Hivite worked to deceive Israel.

a. Being deceived by play-acting.
This is when a person pretends to be someone/something else.

📖 And the inhabitants of Gibeon have heard that which Joshua hath done to Jericho and to Ai, and they work, even they, with subtilty, and go, and <u>feign to be ambassadors</u>, and take old sacks for their asses, and wine-bottles, old, and rent, and bound up, and sandals, old and patched, on their feet, and old garments upon them, and all the bread of their provision is dry -- it was crumbs. Joshua 9:3-5 YLT. ^(Underlined for emphasis)

The Gibeonites feared Israel, and used the ruse of being foreigners to deceive her.

b. Being deceived into making covenant with the world.

📖 And they went to Joshua unto the camp at Gilgal, and said to him, and to the men of Israel, From a far country are we come; and now <u>make a covenant with us</u>. Joshua 9:6 DBY. ^(Underlined for emphasis)

Anytime a Christian dates a non-Christian there is a temptation to make covenant with the world. The dangers of sororities, fraternities, lodges, and secret societies include ungodly oaths and wrongful covenant making.

The Hivites play-acted they were from a distant country, so Israel saw no need to fear them. Commander Joshua did ask a few good questions of the people but made a mistake in not discerning their scheme. A greater mistake was not inquiring of the Lord.

c. Being deceived by promise of blessing.

Many young women have been spoiled by men who promised their love and faithfulness, only to be horribly hurt. Thousands are deceived by dare to be rich schemes because they believe empty promises. Americans now foolishly believe there is such a thing as a "free lunch."

📖 Then the men of Israel took some of their provisions . . . Joshua 9:14a NKJV.

d. Being deceived that one can see the whole picture apart from God.

📖 . . . but they did not ask counsel of the Lord. Josh. 9:14b NKJV.

We have ministered to many who have developed a perhaps healthy mistrust of modern medicine. In their rejection, however, of doctors and hospitals they have fallen into deception of alternative treatments that often do more harm than good. Even though James tells them to call for the elders, confess their faults, and receive healing and prayerful counsel from them, they like to bypass God's safeguards to their own harm.

e. Being deceived by things hard to escape.

Hivite curses and spirits find delight in people who find themselves caught in webs they cannot escape. "Come on, young person, take this, drink this, smoke this, inject this." "It will be fun!" That temporary high often leads to prostituting your own body so you can get your next fix.

📖 And all the princes said to all the assembly, we have sworn unto them by Jehovah the God of Israel, and now we may not touch them. Joshua 9:19 DBY.

Contracts we make with the enemy can be broken, but not without resistance. Israel found herself bound by the curse and deception of the Hivites.

Learning from The Mistakes of the Israelites:

a. They made the mistake of taking the Hivites at their word.

What they heard sounded good. The Hivites promised to be a blessing, not a curse, but the opposite proved true. Remember this before you sign a rent to own contract or sign for a quick loan based on your next paycheck. Believe God – but be discerning of people, especially those who promise you great things, like a ten-fold return if you support their ministry.

b. They made the mistake of taking the Hivites at face value.

This happens time and again. A person finally turns to the Lord. They "acquire the fire" and purpose to do great things for God. And time and again, the devil puts some pretty young woman, or handsome young man into their path, and soon they are head over heels in love with someone who will draw them away from God. Missionary dating never works, but countless young people and adults are led astray in this way. Our friends make us or break us. The Bible says a companion of fools will suffer much harm. The whole name of the Church, "Ecclasia" means called out ones."

c. They questioned the people but did not inquire of the Lord.

The Israelites made their fatal decision by what they saw with their eyes and heard with their ears. They never even asked God what he thought. The same thing often happens when choosing friends, counselors, business partners, and the like. Ask God first!

d. They made a pact with the world.

As apostolic believers, we have a mandate to *go into* all the world, not let all the world *into us!* We are the light and salt of the earth. We need to impact the world by partnering with Jesus for the world rather than partnering with the world. The Bible commands:

📖 Do not be unequally yoked together with unbelievers. For what fellowship has righteousness with lawlessness? And what communion has light with darkness? 2 Corinthians 6:14 NKJV.
(Underlined for emphasis)

Paul asks some rhetorical questions and then summarizes how to be God's people in a polluted world.

📖 and what fellowship to light with darkness? and what concord to Christ with Belial? or what part to a believer with an unbeliever? and what agreement to the sanctuary of God with idols? for ye are a sanctuary of the living God, according as God said -- `I will dwell in them, and will walk among [them], and I will be their God, and they shall be My people, wherefore, come ye forth out of the midst of them, and be separated, saith the Lord, and an unclean thing do not touch, and I -- I will receive you, 2 Corinthians 6:15-17 YLT.
(Underlined for emphasis)

Ways we get caught up in the Hivite spirit:

a. Modern Psychology.

The church has made a contract with the world concerning much of modern psychiatry. We can't understand the difference between light and darkness unless we make a comparison between "God's Say So and Man's Know So."

I was probably in my first or second year of college, with minors in psychology and sociology, when my pastor asked me to minister to a woman who was in terrible shape. I went, armed with everything I was learning in psychology classes. I didn't even take my Bible.

Five years later a man in our church who was president of his company asked me to visit a Vietnam Vet who was such an alcoholic he would have to fire him if things didn't change. This time I went armed only with my Bible and the Holy Spirit. They had already tried everything else. His wife looked me square in the eyes and said "there is no hope for my husband." They had tried counseling, V.A. treatment and a host of other things. I knew the one answer powerful enough to set him free. I introduced him to Jesus and counseled him by the Word of God. He not only got free, he stayed free. He kept his job, had other children, and nearly four decades later remains free.

I am thankful for counselors who are truly Christian in their practice, but I was such a failure in trying to help that woman that I began using the Bible first when ministering. Along with Holy Spirit, the Bible still proves to be the best tool we have to help others.

Jay Adams wrote the book "Competent to Counsel," where he lays out the framework that Christians who know the Word of God and have the Spirit of God are the best counselors available!

b. We used to have the "Criminal Model" for working with Mental Patients.

They were put in prisons because they were considered criminal, rather than mentally ill. A catatonic schizophrenic might stand for hours until someone would change their position.

There are many programs which are much better than the criminal model. Reflecting on how they are served, however, I wonder how much more effective it would be if treatment models would include a biblical model that included deliverance and deep inner healing.

c. The "Mentally Ill Model" for working with mental patients was adopted.

The problem was considered "mental" and as such, they were put in mental institutions and treated for mental illness, as if it were caused by a gene or a virus. I was home supervisor for AIS (Alternative Institutional Services) homes from 1987-1992. The goal was to bring developmentally disabled or mentally ill clients into homes where they could be as normalized as possible. There were blessings and challenges with such thinking. Again, I wonder how much more effective a program would be that includes prayer and spiritual ministry.

d. Transactional Analysis "I'm OK you're OK."

Doctor Thomas Harris, called the super ego the parent, the ego the adult, and the id the child. I took a man from my first church to a professional counselor who was also a Methodist Preacher. I sat with the man during his many sessions as the counselor tried to help the man's super-ego take dominion over his "parent and child," so he could make right decisions as an adult. I didn't know other options back then. Now, in my opinion, salvation, deep healing, and deliverance would have been far more helpful.

e. Freudian and other theories.

Many believe Freud's theory that each person is comprised of an id; ego, and super ego. Wikipedia summarizes thus:

> "the id is the set of uncoordinated instinctual trends; the super-ego plays the critical and moralizing role; and the ego is the organized, realistic part that mediates between the desires of the id and the super-ego. The super-ego can stop one from doing certain things that one's id may want to do."[5]

The wisdom of the world is contrary to what the Bible teaches. As Believers, we have the answer. It is the world that has it backwards. Without God and His Word, there is little hope for transformation. People trained in worldly disciplines offer little hope.

In 1974, I tried counseling an alcoholic using material I learned from college minors in psychology and sociology. My pastor sent me to help a woman who was a desperate alcoholic. I counseled using all the worldly wisdom I possessed. There was no change, even with a prayer to receive Christ. I determined right then to counsel according to the Word and the Spirit of God. Later I was sent to help a Vietnam Vet who was a "helpless" alcoholic. His own wife said there wasn't any help for him. This time I used the Bible and prayer. He was converted and now, thirty years later, remains free from alcohol.

It took me years to understand what the Bible says about deliverance and healing, but now that we are no longer under Hivite deception, we are finally able to release freedom and health to others.

Another major way we get caught up in the ways of Hivite is:

f. Believing real living comes by pleasing the flesh.

Hivite tempts us with "If it feels good, do it." Then, when the guilt of sin begins to ruin our lives, we seek psychology and counseling to relieve the pressure of guilt.

The word "psychology" comes from two Greek words. "Psyche" which is translated "soul or life," and "logos" which is translated "word" as in John 1:1: "In the beginning was the Logos, and the logos was with God, and the logos was God." Believers have the Word of the Soul! The world doesn't! What the world calls life is death, what the world calls death is life. The Prodigal Son, for example, left his Father's place to pursue all his fleshly drives. If it felt good, he did it. He was pleasing his "id" and "ego." But his father said "My son is dead." When his son left those unfulfilling worldly pleasures, and came back to his father's house, The Father said "My son lives again."

Hivite says "please yourself and enjoy life." Jesus taught abundant life comes from dying to the flesh and living for the Lord.

📖 But Jesus answered them, saying, "The hour has come that the Son of Man should be glorified. Most assuredly, I say to you, unless a grain of wheat falls into the ground and dies, it remains alone; but if it dies, it produces much grain. <u>He who loves his life will lose it, and he who hates his life in this world will keep it for eternal life</u>. John 12:23-25 NKJV. ^(Underlined for emphasis)

g. Thinking personal gratification brings satisfaction.

The wisdom from God is pure, holy and virtuous. Heavenly wisdom leads to righteous behavior. But multitudes of people are enticed by the Hivite spirit and believe if they can only get a little more gratification they will be satisfied. That is delusion! A baby will cry and fuss, knowing everything will be just fine if only they can nurse. That's cute – it is the life of a baby. But something is terribly wrong when a teenager or adult thinks everything will be alright if they can only find their next fix.

h.   Thinking Christian life is supposed to be easy.

The Bible says everyone who is godly shall suffer persecution. If we stand tall for Jesus, the world will be against us. No serious Christian will enter ministry thinking they will only have to work on Sundays. No "sent one" will enter business or government believing recognition, success, and increase will be handed to them on a silver platter. Jesus says anyone who puts his hand to the plow and looks back is not fit for the Kingdom of God.

The Bible tells us to work out our salvation with fear and trembling, and whatever we do to work at it with all our heart as working for the Lord not men. Christian life is abundant, but we cannot follow the example of Jesus Christ and expect it to be easy. Rather than being seeker sensitive, we need to be Spirit sensitive.

The Spirit of God leads into battle, not away from it. He leads us to take up the cross, not shun it.

People are deceived by the Hivite spirit. They go from woman to man and man to woman and from woman to woman and man to man, seeking pleasure in what the Bible says brings death. The Hivite spirit always touches death, not life. We must say no to death and yes to life.

i.   Thinking we can flirt with the world.

Jacob's daughter, Dinah flirted with the world, illustrating the Hivite curse.

📖 Now Dinah, the daughter Leah had borne to Jacob, <u>went out to visit the women of the land</u>. When Shechem son of Hamor the Hivite, the ruler of that area, saw her, he took her and <u>raped her</u>. Genesis 34:1-2. ^(Underlined for emphasis)

We minister to many who have been raped. Rape is always wrong, it always dishonors people, and we have great compassion for victims of rape. Demons take advantage of rape, and many, if not most rape victims we minister to have been raped more than once.

Every perpetrator deserves to be punished severely. Without justifying Shechem in anyway, may I ask if you think Dinah put herself in danger by going out to places she shouldn't have gone to spend time with the wrong kind of people? Many victims of rape were at the wrong kind of party, hanging out with the wrong kind of people when they were victimized.

The word Dinah means "judgment" and Hamor means "inflamed." When Dinah went down and partied with the Hivites, she exposed herself to the lust of Hamor who defiled her. Dinah was in the wrong place, doing the wrong thing, with the wrong people when she was raped. Yes, Shechem and his people were justly punished, but Dinah regretted ever getting involved with them.

j. Thinking we can love the world and the Lord at the same time.

Don't think one can love both the world and the Lord. That doesn't work. We are to love people so much we want to influence them for the kingdom for their sakes. We are in the world, but not of the world. We need to invade the world with light, not allow darkness to permeate our lives.

Men, there are ladies where you work and live who will come after you like Potiphar's wife went after Joseph. Run! Ladies, there are men where you live and work who will pursue you like Shechem did Dinah. Run!

📖 Do not love the world or the things in the world. If anyone loves the world, the love of the Father is not in him.1 John 2:15 NKJV.

How We Should Treat the World:

a. Joseph running from temptation.   Genesis 34.

Potiphar's wife must have been a real fox, and she was used to getting her own way. She was good looking, well dressed, rich, and looking for someone who might pay her more attention than her husband did. What did Joseph do when she began to entice him? He made a flight of faith. He was determined to deny himself of all the pleasure he might have gotten from that woman, in order to pursue what God had for him. The Greek translation of the word "escape" means "a flight from this world." Joseph fled!

We need to make the "flight of faith from this world." Instead of running to raves and parties, we should flee them. Instead of running to alcohol, drugs, nicotine, we need to make a flight of faith. God gives us the power to do so!

📖 Through these he has given us his very great and precious promises, so that through them you may participate in the divine nature and <u>escape the corruption in the world caused by evil desires</u>. 2 Peter 1:4 NIV. (Underlined for emphasis)

b. Moses chose eternal blessing over temporary pleasure.

📖 By faith Moses, when he had grown up, refused to be known as the son of Pharaoh's daughter. <u>He chose to be mistreated along with the people of God rather than to enjoy the pleasures of sin for a short time</u>. He regarded disgrace for the sake of Christ as of greater value than the treasures of Egypt, because he was looking ahead to his reward. By faith he left Egypt, not fearing the king's anger; he persevered because he saw him who is invisible. Hebrews 11:24-27 NIV. (Underlined for emphasis)

Moses was in line for greatness in Egypt, but he made the flight of faith. Too many people seek promotion rather than serving Christ. The body of Christ needs a holy desire to be righteous and holy.

c. Noah pursued righteousness rather than man's approval.

📖 This is the account of Noah. Noah was a righteous man, blameless among the people of his time, and he walked with God. Genesis 6:9 NIV.

Noah made the right choice. During this generation, as in the days of Noah, can there be people who are righteous, who will walk before God without sin? How do we get there? One step is walking in victory!

How to Walk in Victory Over the World and The Hivite Spirit:

a. Be filled with the Holy Spirit and be sanctified.

Being filled with the Holy Spirit and fully sanctified, brings freedom from the temptations of this world and the habits that will destroy. We need to take a flight of faith from the haughty "I don't need your help God, I can do it on my own, I will do it in my timing" lie of the Hivite spirit.

Imagine someone driving by in a pickup, when you are lugging 60-pound weight on your back. It they offered you a ride, would you say "No thanks, I can make it?" Pride might refuse help, but humility says "thank you" and climbs in. God has the power to free us from the burden of sin. We need to humble ourselves before God so He will lift us up.

28 promises from Romans 8 for those who will walk by the Holy Spirit and resist Hivite temptation to be worldly:

1. No condemnation.
2. The Spirit of life sets us free.
3. The righteous requirements of the law are met in us.
4. We have our minds set on what the Spirit desires.
5. We are controlled not by the sinful nature, but by the Spirit.
6. The Spirit of God lives in us.
7. Our spirits are alive because of His righteousness.
8. We can say "NO" to the sinful nature.
9. We can put to death the misdeeds of the body.
10. We are filled by the Spirit of God.
11. We do not have a spirit that makes us a slave again to fear.
12. We have the Spirit of sonship and by him we cry, "Abba, Father."
13. The Spirit himself testifies with our spirits that we are God's children.
14. We are heirs of God and co-heirs with Christ.
15. We can we share in his sufferings and in his glory.
16. He will liberate the world from its bondage to decay into glorious freedom.
17. The Spirit helps us in our weakness.
18. The Spirit himself intercedes for us.
19. He who searches our hearts knows the mind of the Spirit.

20. The Spirit helps us do God's entire will.
21. In all things God works for our good.
22. We are predestined to be like Jesus.
23. We are called, justified, glorified.
24. God is for us.
25. God will graciously give us all things. (At least all our needs!)
26. Nothing can condemn us.
27. Nothing can separate us from God.
28. We are more than conquerors.

Breaking Hivite curses and casting down Hivite spirits:

- Father, we confess and repent for where we and our ancestors have given into seduction.
- We confess and repent of all personal and ancestral entrapment to pornography, media and other electronics that have swayed us from godliness and holiness.
- We confess and repent of personal and ancestral partnership with the world and its ways.
- We cast down seduction and command every seducing spirit to leave now. (Expel)
- We break off the spirits of this world and command them to leave. (Expel)
- Jezebel and Ahab - Release us now! (Expel)
- We break every Hivite curse and command Hivite spirits to loose us, now, and go to the feet of Jesus. (Expel)
- Father, we ask you to sanctify us through and through.
- Bring our spirit, soul, and body into perfect alignment we pray.
- In Jesus' name and through His blood. Amen!

Endnotes:

[1]The Seven Mountain Prophecy – Johnny Enlow – Summary Sheet http://www.the7mountains.com/2010/01/24/the-seven-mountain-prophecy-johnny-enlow-summary-sheet/
[2]Sermon: The Spirit of Deception (Hivites)
 http://www.sermoncentral.com/sermons/the-spirit-of-deception-chad-prather-sermon-on-faith-50815.asp
[3]Ads Kampala https://ads-kampala.org/2014/03/05/the-hivite-spirit/
[4] Sermon: The Spirit of Deception (Hivites)

http://www.sermoncentral.com/sermons/the-spirit-of-deception-chad-prather-sermon-on-faith-50815.asp

[5] *Id, ego and super-ego, Wikipedia:*
https://en.wikipedia.org/wiki/Id,_ego_and_super-ego

Further Study:

- Shamah Elim The Hivites, First posted: July 10, 2004. http://shamah-elim.info/hivite.htm
- https://ads-kampala.org/2014/03/05/the-hivite-spirit/ The Andrew Discipleship School – Kampala
- Hivite Spirit Posted Apr 30th 2004, 02:25 by Frontlines Ministries on Prophetic

10 PERIZZITE

Johnny Enlow Summarizes the seven Canaanite spirits and their place of attack on the Seven Mountains of influence. He lists the mountains of influence, and says this about Perizzite:

Mountain of Religion. Perizzites (represent idolatry) are the Enemy of this mountain. They work under the principality of the religious spirit (false worship) to displace the significant authority of Holy Spirit who has the basic mission to model a Holy Spirit infused life and ministry. Revelation 5:12 Key: Honour.[1]

The word Perizzite means unwalled town or unwalled village. The example of the Perizzites is being unwalled or unguarded spiritually. Without roots that go deep, the tree is easily blown over. So it is with Christians who have not taken root and who are unguarded or unwalled in their Christian lives.

Perizzite works with two major religious principalities:
a. Political spirit of religion.

Faisal Malick wrote the excellent book *The Political Spirit* in 2008. It opened my eyes to how political spirits of religion work through political means to hold people and countries in bondage.

Author Faisal Malick uncovers political propaganda masquerading as a quest for the greater good, and unmasks the political spirit behind Islam. The Political Spirit is a sobering, straight forward book that exposes the truth of power and politics. It uncovers the facade of corrupt governing systems and religious hypocrisy by showing you what really drives people to lose their moral compass in the pursuit of power. The political spirit forges alliances with religious and Jezebel spirits to forward a hideous hidden agenda. You can learn to recognize, resist, and defeat The Political Spirit.[2]

b. Corporate spirit of religion.

The corporate spirit of religion works through corporate means to replace worship in spirit and in truth with forms of worship that deny the power of God. Denominations, church boards, or church leaders may use corporate means to coerce people into old wineskins when the Lord is up to something new.

c. There seems to be two divisions of the corporate spirit of religion:

1) The non-Christian division.

This division seeks to keep lost people from coming to salvation. Many cults and false teachers are full of commendable zeal, but are used by Satan to keep people from trusting in Christ alone for salvation.

2) The Christian division.

This division tries to keep people from coming into the fullness of the Holy Spirit. Entire books have been written to warn people not to move into the fullness of Holy Spirit, gifts, or the apostolic mandate. Pam and I have come face to face with this spirit working through people who hate using banners, dancing before the Lord, and singing songs to the Lord, rather than limiting our repertoire to hymns and the like. That spirit was quite busy when Rita Johnson brought her team to Sturgis to ordain me as an apostle and Pam as a prophet/seer. We were actually heckled by immature Christians who shouted out things like "apostasy, heresy, and the like." There was an elder who through a childish fit when we began transitioning worship. He pouted and eventually left the church because songs on the overhead didn't let him follow the tenor line in the hymnal. He was saved and loved Jesus, but was bound by the same corporate spirit of religion he wanted to bind us with.

Perizzite is strongman behind spirits of religion.

In the final chapter I will share how a counterfeit trinity of the queen of heaven, Baal, and leviathan rule over most of the lesser strongmen. I suggest the following prayer before going deeper.

Prayer: Father, in Jesus' Name and by the help of Holy Spirit, we ask you to prepare us to receive the engrafted Word of God, and the God of the Word in fullness. We ask you to cleanse our hearts of unbelief. Free us from doubt and move us from faith to faith and glory to glory. Teach us to wait on you and be renewed by Your Spirit. Fill us increasingly with Your Spirit as we commit to keep in Step with You. Bring us to the point of Spiritual Victory, so what we say will come to pass. Help us build strong walls around our spirits and emotions. Enable our spiritual roots to grow deep. Empower us to win the lost, heal the sick, cast out demons, set captives free, and proclaim the year of your favor. In Jesus' Name, amen.

As we move toward the Promise Land of victorious Christian living, the Devil tries to rob our joy and victory. The pattern and examples given by the Israelites as they moved into the Promise land were recorded so we might learn how to overcome every Canaanite spirit. The craftiest of all these may be Perizzite. This one is after you and me. It wants to hold us captive to a form of religion, rather than loose us to function in the Spirit. Paul targets it in 1 Corinthians 10:12.

📖 So, if you think you are standing firm, be careful that you don't fall! 1 Corinthians 10:12 NIV.

Perizzite would have us be concrete in our faith.

I know concrete is strong and makes great parking lots, but it is hard, set in its ways, and immovable. God wants us to keep in step with the Spirit. Perizzite tempts us to reject new things God is doing in our day. It moves us to worship old wineskins.

Perizzite schemes to keep leaders of old wineskins from supporting leaders of new wine-skins. These people love Jesus and their church. They just don't want things to change, regardless of what God wants. Paul warned us if we think we are right, and figure we have our acts together, to be careful we don't fall. I think of a man whom I dearly loved. He rejected teaching on healing, deliverance, and the like and died much sooner than his family would have liked. I think of another young man whom we truly loved. He rejected our message, and cut us off. He did respond years later when we sent his family a sympathy card when his father committed suicide.

This man stayed in the old wineskin of religion and kept going to the same church for years after we left. The devil doesn't care if we go to church – he just doesn't want us to be the Church of Jesus Christ, doing the things Jesus commissioned us to do.

The Perizzites were one of the older population groups of Palestine and lived in the hill country of Judah. They were an Old Testament nomadic people, much like the Gypsies or circus people of our day. Their roots didn't go deep into rich soil. They moved from place to place and lived in tents or temporary housing.

Perizzite likes boundary makers, Jesus wants us to develop deep roots.

My apostle doesn't want to be my "covering," even though she is. She wants to take the lid off me and our ministry. She doesn't impose boundaries but frees us to follow God. We can have deep roots in Christ and remain stable even when we are moved from one ministry to another. Without deep roots a tree is easily blown over. Perizzite works so Christians won't take root, so they remain unguarded and unwalled in their Christian lives.

Perizzite looks for a breach in the wall.

Encarta Dictionary gives these definitions of breach:
* A failure to obey, keep, or preserve something such as a law, trust, or promise.
* Estrangement, a breakdown in friendly relations.
* A hole in something that is caused by something else forcing its way through.
* A gap that results when somebody or something leaves.[3]

These definitions of breach show how active Perizzite is in modern church life. Too many Believers and churches have breaches in their walls that Satan and his demons pass through. I like the way The Message paraphrases the verse that says a person who does not rule his/her own spirit is like a city whose walls are broken down.

📖 A person without self-control is like a house with its doors and windows knocked out. Proverbs 25:28 MSG.

If you are not in control of your life and circumstances, who is? Don't blame it on "God." He made you in His image; you are sovereign over your own life. As adults, you and I are most responsible for what we let in and keep out of our lives! Deliverance ministers can set you free, but you need to keep yourself free!

Ezekiel gives an end time prophecy, saying when Gog and Magog see unwalled cities, they will say "Let's go down and take their spoils for they at rest." Spiritually this speaks of people whose emotions and will are at rest, making their spirits vulnerable. Magog pictures the devil, seeking weak, un-rooted Christians to devour.

People "at ease in Zion" are not prepared for attack.

If you don't build spiritual walls of protection for yourself and your family through Bible reading, church attendance, prayer and the like, it means you *think* you are dwelling in safety and there is no need for protection. Let me tell you a secret: we are not in heaven yet. We still have an enemy who will strike those who are sleeping.

This happened to King David, the great king, worshipper, and song writer. What a wonderful man of God. He wrote hundreds of worship songs. His heart was after God. God was pleased with him in everything he did, except the matter of Uriah the Hittite and his wife Bathsheba. How could such a godly man fall into the sin of adultery and murder? He was at ease, resting in safety on the wall, when he should have been going to war. He fell out of God's timing and season for his life.

David laid down when he should have been standing! Woe to those who are at ease in Zion! We cannot be at ease, not when we have an enemy out there who is trying to kill, steal and destroy. We can't quit praying, reading, meditating, joining in worship and the Word. If we do, we will fall into temptation like David did.

People with unwalled emotions are weak in spirit.

The god of this age has duped our society into "letting it all hang out." He emphasizes expressing whatever emotions overtake you. If you are angry, "yell, scream, and hit." If you are sad, "drown your sorrows in your beer." If you are happy, "party to your hearts content." If you are full of lust, "sleep with the first person you can." People who are controlled by their emotions are like Humpty Dumpty sitting on a wall, about to take a great fall.

Heathy emotions safeguard our spirit man.

The devil, whom I call "joy-sucker," wants to steal our peace and joy. If he can do that, he immobilizes our spirits, leading to negative reactions. At that point we are unable to pray in the spirit, or resist in the spirit. That means we will end up falling, when God wants us to stand firm, and having done all, continue to stand.

The enemy wants us to lie down in our spirits.

When we carry false guilt or condemnation, it robs our spirits and causes them to be weak and to lie down. Bitterness, anger, jealousy and the like also make our spirits weak. Do you feel like your spirits have been laying down on the job? David did thus for a while.

> When I kept it all inside,
>   my bones turned to powder,
>   my words became daylong groans.
> The pressure never let up;
>   all the juices of my life dried up.
> Then I let it all out;
>   I said, "I'll make a clean breast of my failures to God."
> Suddenly the pressure was gone—
>   my guilt dissolved,
>   my sin disappeared.
> These things add up. Every one of us needs to pray;
>   when all hell breaks loose and the dam bursts
>   we'll be on high ground, untouched. Psalm 32:3-6 MSG.

As soon as David got right in spirit, his body began to mend.

Ongoing grief is a major source that wounds the spirit.

A merry heart does good, like medicine, but a broken spirit dries the bones. Proverbs 17:22 NKJV.

It is normal and healthy to grieve loss, If we maintain hope. If we grieve as those with no hope, it wounds our spirits and makes us weak. Some grieving does more harm than good. When husbands, wives, parents or children grieve because they have expectations of what each other should be like, their grief weakens their spirit.

The secret of a happy life is to yield rights and expectations to God.

Even the best of people let us down at times. The Bible says our expectations are to be from God. He is the One who meets our needs. He may use our families to meet needs, but God is the source! Listen to His advice in Psalm 62:1-2, 5-8.

<u>Truly my soul silently waits for God</u>;
From Him comes my salvation.
[2] <u>He only is my rock and my salvation;</u>
He is my defense;
I shall not be greatly moved.
[5] <u>My soul, wait silently for God alone,</u>
For my expectation is from Him.
[6] He only is my rock and my salvation;
He is my defense;
I shall not be moved.
[7] In God is my salvation and my glory;
The rock of my strength,
And my refuge, is in God.
[8] Trust in Him at all times, you people;
Pour out your heart before Him;
God is a refuge for us. Selah Psalm 62:1-2, 5-8 NKJV.
(Underlined for emphasis)

When we yield our personal rights and expectations to the Lord, we leave the problems in His hands and He begins changing us even as he works on our problems. If we fail to yield our rights and expectations to the Lord, we tend to be angry over real or perceived violations of our rights. Our sinful nature wants to demand its rights, but our spiritual nature knows it is better to yield our expectation to God and trust the Lord work all things together for good.

Do you notice how David's spirit man tells his soul to think, believe, and hope? He comes into right alignment and his spirit commands: "My soul, wait silently for God alone," etc.

Consider the following examples:

When a child or teenager wants something from their parents they don't have the discretionary income to buy, pouting or getting angry seldom change things. It is better to yield those expectations to the Lord. He will either supply what you want or you will learn godliness with contentment and it will be great gain.

Think about getting things done around the house. If you nag, your family will be less prone to want to please. Will that help? But if you truly give your expectation to God and He works on them, things will change. When they do what you want, you will be grateful and praise them. Will that help? Of course it will. Give your expectations to the Lord.

I've met with many men and women who are dissatisfied with their frequency of love life. If they complain to or about their spouse, it drives them to be more distant, and the complainer become crankier and less attractive. Will that help? If they truly yield their rights to the Lord, however, He will minister to you and make you more attractive. Don't you think that will be more helpful than complaining? Give your expectations to the Lord.

Without deep roots, Perizzite will knock you down:

a. Dig your roots deep with prayer.
I memorized a verse on prayer shortly after I was saved.

📖 Until now you have not asked for anything in my name. Ask and you will receive, and your joy will be complete. John 16:24.

I thought about that verse one spring day when I got out of work at 1:00 p.m. I had a great thought. I asked God for a big mess of morel mushrooms. I packed my family in the car and headed to my favorite spot. We didn't find a single mushroom. In my immaturity, I got mad at God, and quoted the John 16:24 back to him. By the time I got to the car, however, I was convicted and confessed my anger and yielded my expectations to him. It was too nice to head to our little home on the other side of the tracks in Hillsdale, so I swung around by a mill which had been closed for years, thinking we might find some asparagus along the railroad track. I couldn't park near the tracks so drove a little further to some firm ground. We stepped out of the car and there were huge yellow mushrooms everywhere – a couple of paper grocery sacks full!

We have learned we accomplish more in prayer than we ever could by griping, complaining, or even by hard work.

b. Dig your roots deep in Jesus.

I'm not talking about religion or works based living, but in Jesus Himself. He said:

📖 Abide in Me, and I in you. As the branch cannot bear fruit of itself, unless it abides in the vine, neither can you, unless you abide in Me. "I am the vine, you are the branches. He who abides in Me, and I in him, bears much fruit; for without Me you can do nothing. If anyone does not abide in Me, he is cast out as a branch and is withered; and they gather them and throw them into the fire, and they are burned. If you abide in Me, and My words abide in you, you will ask what you desire, and it shall be done for you. By this My Father is glorified, that you bear much fruit; so you will be My disciples. John 15:4-8.

In the 1970's and 80's I became far too religious. I was a religious workaholic, trying to prove my worth to God and the congregation I pastored. I went through the motions of Bible reading, prayer lists, worship, and other things good Christians are supposed to do—but my relationship with Jesus withered.

After failing miserably in 1987, I started seeking Jesus Himself. I put away my King James Scholfied study Bible, and bought one that had very few notes. I wanted to get closer to Jesus and the pure Word of God. I never want to slip back into religious ways. Now, I try to walk several times a week, simply to be with Jesus. When I miss a few days, I feel like my roots are searching for living water but can't quite reach them. I need Jesus. I quote Psalm 91 back to the Lord as I go to sleep every night. I choose to dwell in the shelter of the Most High and rest in the shadow of the Almighty.

c. Dig your roots deep into the Word of God and the God of the Word.

Either God's Word will keep you from sin or sin will keep you from God's Word. Over twenty years ago, Pam and I decided to read the Bible together every morning. We get up, make coffee, and look into the Old and New Testaments before we shower or go to work. Sometimes we have to get up at 4:00 a.m. to do that, but we want our roots to be deep in God and His Word.

d. Dig your roots deep in the Body of Christ.

I don't believe it is possible to be a good Christian while disconnected from the church. When I say "church," I am talking about the Body of Christ where ever and whenever it meets. The symbolism of Jesus being the body, and individual Christians being the eyes, ears, arms, legs, etc., proves how essential it is to stay connected to each other. Pam's hands do things with the piano that are simply amazing to me. But if those hands were disconnected from her body, they could do nothing. So it is with Christians who are disconnected from the body of believers.

e. Dig your roots deep in fellowship.

Church is great, but we also need fellowship beyond the church. I am grateful for my prayer partner and for people who stop by occasionally to see how I am doing. I always feel stronger after I've talked with Ed, or Clarence, or Marge, or Dick, or Lorraine, or David, or Andrew or others who care for me like I do for them. This is biblical. The writer of Hebrews understood this need.

📖 And let us consider one another in order to stir up love and good works, not forsaking the assembling of ourselves together, as is the manner of some, but exhorting one another, and so much the more as you see the Day approaching. Hebrews 10:24-25 NKJV.

Types of people who followed Jesus:

a. Doubters and rejecters.

They stayed just close enough to complain. They were part of the problem, but not part of the solution. They were upset Jesus healed the sick, especially on the Sabbath, but they personally had no power or compassion to heal the sick.

b. Casual attenders.

They stayed close enough to witness some miracles and catch some blessings, but for the most part they were of the church but not the church. John Maxwell calls this group the 80% of the people who do only 10% of the work. This reminds me of something Dick Bolley once read to our church.

There was an important job to be done and Everybody was asked to do it. Everybody was sure that Somebody would do it. Anybody could have done it, but Nobody did it. Somebody got angry about that! After all, it was Everybody's job. Everybody thought Anybody could do it, but Nobody realized that Everybody wouldn't do it. It ended up that Everybody blamed Somebody because Nobody had wound up doing what Anybody could have done!

c. Regular Attenders. Nine of the 12 disciples made this up this group.

These people were "in" the ministry. They were doing good works in Jesus' Name. They not only saw Jesus' miracles and blessings, they too healed the sick and cast out some demons. John Maxwell says 20% of the people in a church typically do 80% of the work. The regular attenders were part of the 20% who did the most for God.

d. Intimate inner circle.

James, Peter, and John went beyond just serving Jesus. They knew His heart. Because of their closeness, they witnessed Jesus' transfiguration when he met with Moses and Elijah on the mountain. More than anyone else, they knew what Jesus was really up to.

The inner circle moved the magic mile from being servants to being friends of Jesus.

Jesus wants us to abide in Him so He can abide in us. True Christianity is more about *being* than *doing*. Unfortunately, too many Christians are more caught up in signs and wonders than they are in the wonder of God's Son.

As a deliverance minister, I notice a scheme of the devil to take enthusiastic young believers and thrust them into ministries of signs and wonders. It seems exciting for a while, but they're often like Humpty Dumpty. They take a great fall, and all the King's horses and King's men can't put them together again. They failed to develop character before showing off their gifts, and anointing for signs and wonders. I think of two promising young men who did short time missions and saw God work mighty wonders through them. They became proud and no longer saw the need to submit to authority. They both ended up terribly broken. One actually thought he heard God tell him to steal an empty truck running at a convenience shop. He was so sure of himself after casting demons out of people, he followed a deceptive voice and ended up first in jail, and then in a mental ward.

I memorized John Chapters 14 and 15 years ago. The truth of Jesus' words invite us to move beyond servanthood to intimacy with Him.

📖 You are my friends if you do what I command. <u>I no longer call you servants, because a servant does not know his master's business. Instead, I have called you friends</u>, for everything that I learned from my Father I have made known to you. You did not choose me, but I chose you and appointed you so that you might go and bear fruit—fruit that will last—and so that whatever you ask in my name the Father will give you. John 15:14-16 NIV. (Underlined for emphasis)

Ask yourself:

☐ Have I been caught off guard because I've been at "ease in Zion?"
☐ Do I have "unwalled" emotions that catch me off guard?
☐ Do I feel weak in soul or spirit?
☐ Have my roots been so shallow I am easily blown away?
☐ Do I hunger for deeper roots in: prayer, Jesus, Bible reading, and Body Life?
☐ Have I been attacked by Perizzite spirits?
☐ Am I ready to defeat them?

Breaking off Perizzites:

⸸ Father, we confess and repent of personal and generational idolatry and forms of religion that deny the power and presence of the Lord.
⸸ We confess and repent of personal and generational places and ways we have resisted, quenched or grieved Holy Spirit.
⸸ We confess and repent of personal and generational luke-warmness.
⸸ We confess and repent of being unguarded spiritually.
⸸ We ask Holy Spirit to fill us and displace all religion and idolatry.
⸸ We cast down:
　⸸ Political spirits of religion.
　⸸ Every form of religion that denies the power of God.

꙰ Corporate spirits of religion.

꙰ And any other spirit of religion that is attached to my life, my family or my church! (Expel)

꙰ In Jesus' name, we bind the strongman Perizzite and demolish his strongholds.

꙰ We command Perizzite spirits to leave us now, in Jesus' Name. (Expel)

꙰ We cast down the Perizzite strongman in Jesus' Name. (Expel)

꙰ Father, we draw near to You, knowing You will draw near to us.

꙰ Let us walk in Spirit and in truth.

꙰ Today we receive, by faith, Your offer to be friends with Jesus. Amen.

Endnotes:

[1]The Seven Mountain Prophecy – Johnny Enlow – Summary Sheet
http://www.the7mountains.com/2010/01/24/the-seven-mountain-prophecy-johnny-enlow-summary-sheet/
[2]Malick, Faisal: *The Political Spirit.*
[3]Encarta Dictionary: English (North America)

11 COUNTERFEIT TRINITY OF BAAL

Have you noticed you can read through the Bible time and again, and suddenly words or concepts jump out you have never noticed before? I've read through the Bible dozens of times but recently the name "Baal" has jumped out at me.

The name Baal is used by itself or in hyphenated forms in at least 136 verses. The Bible Gateway Topical Index gives 75 entries for Baal.

Tommie Femrite said America's ruling principalities are the spirits of religion (i.e. the Queen of Heaven) and the Antichrist Spirit. Dutch Sheets and John Benefiel say Baal is the strong man of America. I believe these are all linked together in a counterfeit trinity.

Baal manifests as a false (counterfeit) trinity:

a. Baal
Baal goes by many other names and has his name joined to others.

b. Queen of heaven
She too, goes by many names including Jezebel "Jezebaal" which combines the names Jezebel and Baal.

c. Leviathan
Let me share the word origin and history for leviathan:

"sea monster, sea serpent," also regarded as a form of Satan, from Late Latin leviathan, from Hebrew livyathan "dragon, serpent, huge sea animal," of unknown origin, perhaps related to liwyah "wreath," from root l-w-h- "to wind, turn, twist." Of powerful persons or things from c.1600.[1] (Underlined for emphasis)

Baal is a master at disguise and has many names.

Jan van der Crabben stated the following in an article published on August 3, 2011:

Ba'al (Hebrew בעל, Ba'l, 'lord;" Greek Βῆλος) was the title of several Canaanite deities. The word "Ba'al" can be translated as <u>"lord," "owner," "master," or "husband," and referred to a group of deities</u> venerated in the Levant. Some of these deities were also known under different names (e.g., the storm god Hadad of Aleppo), in which case "Ba'al" was a title; in other cases, "Ba'al" appears to have been a name. The oldest references to him are personal names from the third millennium BCE.[2] (Underlined for emphasis)

Paul warned the Church to watch out for deception.

For such people are false apostles, deceitful workers, masquerading as apostles of Christ. And no wonder, for <u>Satan himself masquerades as an angel of light</u>. It is not surprising, then, if his servants also masquerade as servants of righteousness. Their end will be what their actions deserve. 2 Corinthians 11:13-15 NIV. (Underlined for emphasis)

Some of Baal's names:

From *Hitchcock's Bible Names* – under dictionaries in Bible Gateway.[3] Combined with added thoughts from Easton's Bible Dictionary in Bible Gateway.[4]

a. Baal. master; lord.[3]

Easton adds: "The name appropriated to the <u>principal male god of the Phoenicians</u>." [4] (Underlined for emphasis)

b. Baal-berith. idol of the covenant.[3]

Think of the many false covenants and vows people make to ungodly societies and lodges. Easton's adds their definition of Baal-berith:

"covenant lord, the name of the god worshipped in Shechem after the death of Gideon (<u>Judg. 8:33</u>; <u>9:4</u>). In 9:46 he is called simply "the god Berith." The name <u>denotes the god of the covenant into which the Israelites entered with the Canaanites, contrary to the command of Jehovah</u> (Ex. 34:12), when they began to fall away to the worship of idols.[4] (Underlined for emphasis)

c. Baal-gad. idol of fortune or felicity.[3]

Easton's adds: <u>lord of fortune</u>, or troop of Baal, a Canaanite city in the valley of Lebanon at the foot of Hermon, hence called Baal-hermon (Judge. 3:3; 1 Chr. 5:23), near the source of the Jordan (Josh. 13:5; 11:17; 12:7). It was the most northern point to which Joshua's conquests extended. It probably derived its name from the worship of Baal. Its modern representative is Banias.[4] (Underlined for emphasis)

d. Baal-hermon. possessor of destruction or of a thing cursed.[3]

Some people have things that last forever. Their cars keep running well for over 200,000 miles. Their clothes keep their freshness far longer than normal. Their appliances and electronics seem to last forever. For others, the opposite is true. It may be Baal-hermon is involved.

e. Baal-meon. idol or master of the house.[3]

Baal-meon tries to takes over dominion of the house. This is sad because older homes which have been defiled by their inhabitants, or new homes defiled by their builders or neighborhoods may try to master the home until someone evicts Baal-meon.

f. Baal-peor. master of the opening.[3]

(Eaton's adds: <u>lord of the opening, a god of the Moabites</u> (Num. 25:3; 31:16; Josh. 22:17), <u>worshipped by obscene rites</u>. So called from Mount Peor, where this worship was celebrated, the Baal of Peor. The Israelites fell into the worship of this idol (Num. 25:3, 5, 18; Deut. 4:3; Ps. 106:28; Hos. 9:10).[4] (Underlined for emphasis)

Consider how Baal-peor has used Clinton & Obama to open doors to sexual perversion in our nation. Bill Clinton, while president of the United States, opened the door to sexual perversion by his improprieties with Monica Lewinski. Open door are not always God's will. The Obama administration open the floodgates to further prevision by opening doors to same gender marriage. Baal-peor lord's over such opening until God's people begin to forcibly advance His Kingdom against Baal's rule.

g. Baal-perazim. god of divisions.[3]

Easton's adds: <u>Baal having rents, bursts, or destructions,</u> the scene of a victory gained by David over the Philistines (<u>2 Sam. 5:20</u>; <u>1 Chr. 14:11</u>).[4] (Underlined for emphasis)

Many pastors, including the one writing this, have experienced Absalom's who have looked good, been very gifted, but ended up bringing division because they have not carried the pastor's heart or vision. Baal-perazim loves to crush pastors and divide churches by people who have contrary vision.

h. Baal-shalisha. the god that presides over three; the third idol.[3]

Here I see a counterfeit trinity rising up to usurp the roll of God the Father, God the Son, and God the Holy Spirit.

i. Baal-tamar. master of the palm-tree.[3]

Easton's adds: <u>lord of palm trees</u>, a place in the tribe of Benjamin near Gibeah of Saul (<u>Judg. 20:33</u>). <u>It was one of the sanctuaries or groves of Baal</u>.[4] (Underlined for emphasis)

j. Baal-zebub. god of the fly.

Easton's adds: <u>fly-lord, the god of the Philistines at Ekron</u> (<u>2 Kings 1:2</u>, 3, <u>16</u>). This name was given to the god because he was supposed to be able to avert the plague of flies which in that region was to be feared. He was consulted by Ahaziah as to his recovery.[4] (Underlined for emphasis)

Flies refer to lies that fly about. The Father of Lies is busy when people spread opinions or lies about others in ministry. That is one reason we encourage people to go on a 30-day negative word fast in the Basic Building Blocks Seminar.

k. Baal-zephon. the idol or possession of the north; hidden; secret.[3]

The word "occult" literally means clandestine, hidden, or secret. Secrecy is not a value in the Kingdom of God, but the kingdom of darkness uses secrecy to hold people in bondage.

l. Baalah. her idol; she that is governed or subdued; a spouse.[3]

Baalah links to false, dictatorial, or abusive understanding of submission versus true view of biblical submission. This almost always leads to suppression of women. I think Satan hates women because Jesus was born of a woman. Ephesians 5:15-6:10, rightly understood, does not suppress women or children. It shows the responsibilities of leaders submitting to their follower's need, and followers submitting to their leader's lead.

m. Baalath. a rejoicing; our proud lord.

The epitome of pride is when people put what they think of what God says, that's why I wrote the book *God's Say So versus Man's Know So*. A week before writing this a large west Michigan city celebrated "Gay Pride Week." What's next? Child abusers pride week?

n. Baalath-beer. subjected pit.[3]

I don't think "beer" here has anything to do with drunkenness but applies to the "pits" so many people have found themselves in when they need deliverance. They need help to break control of Baal. Easton's Bible Dictionary - under dictionaries in Bible Gateway[4] gives a few more thoughts on Baal that are worth looking at[4]:

o. Baal is identified with Molech (Jer. 19:5).

Easton's says:

It was known to the Israelites as Baal-peor (Num. 25:3; Deut. 4:3), was worshipped till the time of Samuel (1 Sam 7:4), and was afterwards the religion of the ten tribes in the time of Ahab (1 Kings 16:31-33; 18:19, 22). It prevailed also for a time in the kingdom of Judah (2 Kings 8:27; comp. 11:18; 16:3; 2 Chr. 28:2), till finally put an end to by the severe discipline of the Captivity (Zeph. 1:4-6). The priests of Baal were in great numbers (1Kings 18:19), and of various classes (2 Kings 10:19). Their mode of offering sacrifices is described in 1 Kings 18:25-29.[Ibid]

In March, 2016 several articles exposed a group which intended to build a statue or monument to Baal in New York City. That has not yet been done, to my knowledge, but there is already a monument to Baal there. We will look at that later.

p. The sun-god, under the general title of Baal, or "lord."
Easton's explains this further:
The sun-god was the chief object of worship of the Canaanites. Each locality had its special Baal, and the various local Baals were summed up under the name of Baalim, or "lords." Each Baal had a wife, who was a colourless reflection of himself. [Ibid]

q. Baal-zephon Baalbec called by the Greeks Heliopolis.
Easton again sheds like on Baal-zephon Baalbec saying about it:
i.e., "the city of the sun," because of its famous Temple of the Sun, has by some been supposed to be Solomon's "house of the forest of Lebanon" (1 Kings 7:2; 10:17; 2 Chr. 9:16); by others it is identified with Baal-gad (q.v.). It was a city of Coele-Syria, on the lowest declivity of Anti-Libanus, about 42 miles north-west of Damascus. It was one of the most splendid of Syrian cities, existing from a remote antiquity. After sustaining several sieges under the Moslems and others, it was finally destroyed by an earthquake in 1759. Its ruins are of great extent. [Ibid (Underlined for emphasis)]

r. Baalim plural of Baal; images of the god Baal (Judg. 2:11; 1 Sam. 7:4) [Ibid (Emphasis mine)]
Smith's Bible Names Dictionary - under dictionaries in Bible Gateway says of Baal:[5]

The supreme male divinity of the Phoenician and Canaanitish nations, as Ashtoreth was their supreme female divinity. Some suppose Baal to correspond to the sun and Ashtoreth to the moon; others that Baal was Jupiter and Ashtoreth Venus. There can be no doubt of the very high antiquity of the worship of Baal. It prevailed in the time of Moses among the Moabites and Midianites, (Numbers 22:41) and through them spread to the Israelites. (Numbers 25:3-18; 4:3) In the times of the kings it became the religion of the court and people of the ten tribes, (1 Kings 16:31-33; 18:19,22) and appears never to have been permanently abolished among them. (2 Kings 17:16) Temples were erected to Baal in Judah, (1 Kings 16:32) and he was worshipped with much ceremony. (1 Kings 18:19,26-28; 2 Kings 10:22) The attractiveness of this worship to the Jews undoubtedly grew out of its licentious character. We find this worship also in Phoenician colonies. The religion of the ancient British islands much resembled this ancient worship of Baal, and may have been derived from it. Nor need we hesitate to regard the Babylonian Bel, (Isaiah 46:1) or Beaus, as essentially identical with Baal, though perhaps under some modified form. The plural, Baalim, is found frequently, showing that he was probably worshipped under different compounds, among which appear—5 (Emphasis mine)

Baal is executer of Lucifer's will as Jesus is executor of the Father's will.

Baal, also called "Bel," as seen in the following verse, does Lucifer's (Satan's) will. He is committed to steal, kill, and destroy at his master's command.

📖 I will punish Bel (Baal) in Babylon and make him spew out what he has swallowed. The nations will no longer stream to him. And the wall of Babylon will fall. Jeremiah 51:44.

If you look "Bel" up in Bible dictionaries they will tell you it is another name for Baal. He continually tries to sway people from God's will.

Baal is the god behind covenant breaking within marriage, church, business, and life.

Paul warns how Christians can unknowingly participate with demons and principalities like Baal:

📖 Do I mean then that food sacrificed to an idol is anything, or that an idol is anything? No, but the sacrifices of pagans are offered to demons, not to God, and <u>I do not want you to be participants with demons</u>. You cannot drink the cup of the Lord and the cup of demons too; you cannot have a part in both the Lord's table and the table of demons. 1 Corinthians 10:19-21. ^(Underlined for emphasis)

Biblical indicators Baal is at work:

As I write things like this I pray protection and research multiple websites and sources. I always try to give proper credit to where I receive information, but unfortunately, I honestly cannot find the source of these Bible indicators that Baal is at work. I looked at each of the Scriptures listed but only include their references.

a. Confusion, battling between multiple opinions, indecision. Num. 22:36-41.
b. Sexual sin and perversion. Numbers 25:1-5.
c. Deception and disease. Numbers 25:17-18.
d. Death and destruction. Deuteronomy 4:2-4.
e. Lost generations. Judges 2:10-12.

Here you might consider the "Me" generation for Baal is all about me, myself and I. Or consider the "nones" who have no spiritual connection, or the Millennials who do not accept the Word as absolute truth.

f. Religious confusion and plurality of gods. Judges 2:12-14.

India is the most religious country I've visited. The route we traveled had shrines to different gods set up in about every seventh lot we passed.

g. Evil doing. Judges 3:6-8.
h. Hostility toward true believers. Judges 6:31.
i. Prostitution, sex trafficking, and whoredom. Judges 8:32-34.
j. Disloyalty. Judges 8:35.
k. Backsliding. Judges 10:6.
l. Increasing wickedness. 1 Kings 16:31.
m. Unequally yoked. 1 Kings 16:31-33.
n. Accuses and/or blames the saints. 1 Kings 18:17-19.
o. Self-mutilation and cutting and religious frenzy. 1 Kings 18:28.

We have seen dozens of teens and older people, mostly female, who are driven to cut themselves. Their pain and need is real, but Baal tempts them to self-destruct.

    p.   Divination. 2 Kings 1:1-3.

        Many fine Christians who love Jesus disagree with me here, but current fascination with mediums, Harry Potter, Sorcery, and an increasing number of shows about crossing over, speaking to the dead, etc., have their roots in Baal.

    q.   Idolatry. 2 Kings 17:16.

    r.   Wrong worship, including of "mother earth." 2 Kings 23:5.

        God created man to steward the earth, but there is a danger when the focus of Earth Day becomes worship of the earth and/or mother earth.

    s.   Weak leadership. Jeremiah 2:7-9.

    t.   Sacrifice of children, including abortion. Jeremiah 19:5,32:35.

        Wrongful shedding of blood brings curse on the land. It always has and always will. Baal lures people into what is convenient where God calls people to what is right.

    u.   False prophecy. Jeremiah 23:25-27.

    v.   Vile and shameful. Hosea 9:10.

    w.   Depression and feelings of isolation. Romans 11:3-5.

    x.   Cannot draw near to or hear the Lord. Zephaniah 3:2.

    y.   Wild weekends and unholy holidays. Hosea 2:2-13.

    z.   Asherah poles. 2 Chronicles 33:3. (totem poles)

        Asherah is the name of a sensual Canaanite goddess Astarte, the feminine of the Assyrian Ishtar. Its symbol was the stem of a tree deprived of its boughs, and rudely shaped into an image, and planted in the ground. It was easy to give an "alphabet's worth" of Baal's characteristics – are there are more, many more. As we look at them its apparent that Baal's culture is in North America.

Are all members of the false trinity found in America?

A.   Is Baal manifest in America? (Picture)[7]

1) **Obelisks.** ob·e·lisk. I pray protection and share from an
   Illuminati article.

An Egyptian style obelisk called the Washington
Monument was built in the District of Columbia in 1884. This
enormous phallic monstrosity celebrates one of the most
deceptive Freemasons to ever walk the Earth: General George
Washington. . . .
   The obelisk itself remains the tallest stone structure in the
world today. In 1848, a Fourth of July dedication of the
monument was hosted by local Freemasons and the obelisk's
cornerstone was laid in typical Masonic fashion.[6]

I used to prayer walk through a cemetery a lot when we lived in
town. Our cemeteries have a lot of Obelisks. One cold day before
daylight I was wearing a camouflaged hooded coat. I was praying
around a tall obelisk when I walked into the path of a jogger who took
off so fast I couldn't identify him or her. Obelisks are phallic symbols
of the male sex organ. Consider this: article:

Why is the Obelisk usually erected in front of or near a
Dome building in all ancient cultures? The Dome represents
the Womb, thus we have in the White House an Oval Office
(woman reproductive organs, ovaries) - the energies of the
Moon. The Washington Monument or Obelisk is the Erect
Penis - the energies of the Sun. This is where reproduction and
procreation takes place (laws, bills, etc are passed). These are
highly Masonic symbols of an ancient occult religion that goes
back for thousands of years and yet quietly practiced in plain
sight today.
   Phallic worship is the worship of the erect penis, this is
what constantly got ancient Israel in trouble. The only symbol

for Baal worship was the erect penis or obelisk. Here is an Old Testament passage that tells of Jehu destroying the phallic images after killing those that encouraged phallic worship. "They hauled out the sacred phallic stone from the temple of Baal and pulverized it. They smashed the Baal altars and tore down the Baal temple. It's been a public toilet ever since. And that's the story of Jehu's wasting of Baal in Israel." 2 Kings 10:26-28 The Message Bible.[7]

The largest upright phallus of the SUN in the world is the George Washington monument in Washington D.C., the capital city of the United States of America. Its dimension at its base is 55.5 ft. wide by 55.5 ft. long, with a height 555 ft. high. If you add those three measurements the sum is 666.

2) The all-Seeing Eye.

This eye in the triangle on our dollar bill represents occult spiritual sight, inner vision, higher knowledge, and insight in occult mysteries. It is the Masonic eye of Horus. Let me read from the article Illuminati/Freemasonry/Satanic Symbolism:[8]

The Udjat eye represents the eye of the god Horus. He was a solar god and was represented by a falcon or a falcon headed god.

Horus, the son of Isis and of Osiris, was a god whose attributes appealed strongly to the Egyptians from one end of Egypt to the other.

ALL-SEEING EYE -- The All-seeing eye originated in Egypt in those Satanic Mysteries which God physically judged during the time of Moses, when he lead the Israelites out of the land by the mighty hand of God. The All-Seeing Eye was representative of the omniscience of Horus, the Sun God, (Magic Symbols, by Frederick Goodman, p. 103, Satanic symbols book). As one Masonic book says, "These considerations lead us to an interesting topic, the Eye of Mind or the Eye of Horus ... and conveying the idea of the 'All seeing Eye'. The end set before the Egyptian neophyte was illumination, that is to be 'brought to light'. The Religion of Egypt was the Religion of the Light." (Thomas Milton Stewart, The Symbolism of the Gods of the Egyptians and the Light They Throw on Freemasonry, London, England, Baskerville Press, Ltd., 1927, p. 5)

Anyone who knows their Scripture and thinks of themselves as "Christian" should feel right now like they have been slapped alongside their head with a two-by-four! This Masonic author has just told you that the Light to which Masons constantly refer, and toward which they are to constantly move, is the Religion of Horus! This is damning, because in Egyptian Mythology, Horus IS Lucifer (Former Satanist, William Schnoebelen, Masonry: Beyond The Light, p. 197) SYMBOLS PROVE INVISIBLE FRATERNITY OF FREEMASONRY IS SATANIC!

http://www.theforbiddenknowledge.com/hardtruth/sy mbolism_index.htm[8]

There are dozens of other symbols of Baal in our land. More telling than the symbols, however, are the behaviors of lawlessness, sexual perversion, increasing persecution of Christians who are willing to stand for Biblical Morality and the like.

B. Is the Queen of heaven manifest in America?

The sun god, Isis, Jezebel, etc.. are all manifestations of the Queen of Heaven. The queen of heaven also manifests as Astarte, Ishtar, Columbia, and Jezebel. Jezebel's name ends with "Bel," which we've already learned is another name for Baal.

Beginning and End has a startling article on how Jezebel is working in America titled: *Beyonce Channels the Spirit of Jezebel in Illuminati "Ghost/Haunted Video"*

Pop superstar Beyonce caused a media frenzy with the release of her secret self-titled visual album, "Beyonce." The album which includes a number of images and videos has one video in particular that is deeply disturbing. In the video for her song "Ghost/Haunted", Beyonce invokes much of the imagery that launched her career into superstardom: over sexuality and occult symbolism. The video is emblematic of much of pop music today as it seeks to lead people away from God and into sinful rebellion.[9]

Isis is an ancient sun God, picture below:[10]

1) Anytime you see rays, like rays of the sun, pointing off a statue or picture, you are seeing intentional, overt, or ignorant display of the queen of heaven.

This is even true in religious pictures which show such rays radiating from the heads of Christian symbols. Many religious pictures Think of this in context of the spirits of religion we discussed earlier and how they try to keep unsaved people from getting saved, and saved people from being filled and anointed for signs and wonders that point to the Son Jesus.

Let me show you a picture of one of the queen of heaven's most famous statues.

Right Wing Watches shared this in an internet article:

Libertas is also called the Freedom Goddess, Lady Freedom, the Goddess of Liberty. You know there's a statue in New York harbor called the Statue of Liberty. You know where we got it from? French Free Masons. Listen folks that is an idol, a demonic idol, right there in New York harbor. People say, 'well no it's patriotic.' What makes it patriotic? Why is it? It's a statue of a false goddess, the Queen of Heaven. We don't get liberty from a false goddess folks, we get our liberty from Jesus Christ and that Statue of Liberty in no way glorifies Jesus Christ. There is no connection whatsoever. So I'm just telling you we practice idolatry in America in ways that we don't even recognize.[11]

Jezebel (note the "Baal" at the end of her name) manifests the work of Baal and the queen of heaven. Lest you think I am picking on women, both men and women can have a Jezebel spirit.

Characteristics of Jezebel include:

a) Seduction, Deceiver. Manipulator,
b) Man-Hater, Rebellious, Power-hungry
c) Super achiever, Jealous, Queen Bee
d) Perfectionist, Possessive, Self-pitying
e) Lustful (for sex and power), Curses
f) Superiority Complex, Bitter and Resentful
g) Pretends to love children but uses them as weapons
h) Back-stabber, Bitterness and Resentment
i) Thinks it's all about her.

Do you see any evidence of Jezebel in America?

C. Is Leviathan manifest in America?

There are a lot of photos of Leviathan on the web. I always pray protection before looking at such things. I include one taken from Stock Photo Images Free/ dreamstime.com

Isaiah refers to Leviathan as the twisted serpent. It sneaks up on its prey, snatches it, holds it under water and twists the life out of it so it can rot and later be consumed. Our guide in Namibia showed us intact skeletons of springbuck and impalas along the shore where a lake had dried up. He explained how crocodiles would catch animals coming to drink, pull them under the water and twist them around until their life was gone. After letting them rot for weeks, the crocodiles would lick the skeletons clean.

📖 In that day the Lord with His severe sword, great and strong, will punish Leviathan the fleeing serpent, <u>Leviathan that twisted serpent</u>; and He will slay the reptile that is in the sea. Isaiah 27:1 NKJV. (Underlined for emphasis)

📖 [13] You divided the sea by Your strength; You broke the heads of the sea serpents in the waters. [14] You broke the heads of Leviathan in pieces, And gave him as food to the people inhabiting the wilderness. Psalm 74:13-14 NKJV.

📖 ²⁶There the ships sail about; There is that Leviathan Which You have made to play there. Psalm 104:26 NKJV

📖 In that day the Lord with His severe sword, great and strong, Will punish Leviathan the fleeing serpent, Leviathan that twisted serpent; And He will slay the reptile that is in the sea. Isaiah 27:1. NKJV

📖 ¹³He breathes, and ·the sky clears [he makes the heavens beautiful]. His hand ·stabs [slays] the fleeing ·snake [serpent; C Leviathan, another sea monster representing chaos; 3:8; Is. 27:1]. Job 26:13 Expanded Bible.

📖 See Job 41:1-34 for further insight.

Signs Leviathan is at work:

a. Behind severe problems with Bible reading and spiritual goals.
b. Restricts worship.
c. Learning difficulties with children, including reading. Leviathan connected through family curse. (This curse should be broken for generations and any destroy legal rights and/or satanic schematics must be brought down.)
d. Blocks, prevents revival.
e. Pride and stiffness in neck and shoulder. Job 41:22.
f. Rebellious pride: "Just see what the Lord gives you." Not admitting need when receiving prayer.
g. Deliverance brings radical change in outlook and growth.
h. Many who fight deliverance ministry are under Leviathan's spell.
i. Also called Constellation of the Dragon or Orion. (Here the seven stars represent demonic angels.)
j. IN CASTING OUT: 7 demons stars of Orion: cast out by name of stars: Betelgeuse, Saiph, Bellatrix, Rigel, Alnitak, Alnilam, Mintaka.
k. Often Egyptian spirit (spirit of worldliness) works with Leviathan.
l. Leviathan burrows in the self of man. (Kingdom of self)
m. Leviathan means to twine, unite, and to remain. Root word means to bend or twist.

Leviathan is a marine serpent believed to lie in wait in harbors!

There is a strong evil spirit named Leviathan. There are many good books and teaching concerning him, which go beyond the scope of this seminar. I encourage those with an interest to prayerfully study them.

Leviathan's primary works:

a) **Leviathan manifests through pride "being chief of all creation."**

Job 41 describes this spirit as "king over all the children of pride."

📖 He beholds every high thing; <u>He is king over all the children of pride</u>." Job 41:34 NKJV. (Underlined for emphasis)

"Pride" and "hide" rhyme, and pride hides from its possessor. Pride nearly destroyed me in the 1980's and would have had God not mercifully humbled me.

📖 It was you who split open the sea by your power; you broke the heads of the monster in the waters. Psalm 74:13 NIV.

b) **Leviathan is pictured with multiple heads.**

Do you see pride at work in America's seven mountains or pillars of influence?

The seven mountains include: business, government, media, arts and entertainment, education, family, and religion. Do you see how Leviathan uses pride to kill, steal, and destroy people in each of these pillars of society? It is interesting that pride is one of the seven deadly sins (Proverbs 6:16-19) Leviathan uses to bring destruction and loss to every pillar of society.

c) **One of Leviathan's jobs is to block deliverance.**

Why do you think far more women than men pursue deliverance appointments? Why do leaders, including church leaders, often think deliverance is beneath them? If Leviathan can block deliverance through pride he can use God's word to bring the judgment of demonization upon leader, like he did with King Saul, because God opposes the proud (James 4:6). Our greatest defense against Leviathan is to humble ourselves before the Lord so He will lift us up (James 4:10).

We have the big three of the false trinity to stand against, and we must take our stand. I just happened to read one of John Maxwell's Leadership Promises - *Be Willing to Stand Be Willing to Stand Up* on October 5, 2015 the day I wrote this.

"Hear me, O Lord, hear me, that this people may know that You are the Lord God, and that You have turned their hearts back to You again." 1 Kings 18:37

The prophet Elijah knew about the idolatry of Israel and the wickedness of King Ahab. He knew the time for judgment had arrived. And he also knew that drought and famine were about to devastate Israel. He knew because he himself had announced God's judgment.

This all took place during a very sad time in the history of Israel, when the people had all but turned their backs on God and their king sinned openly and boldly. Elijah, consumed with holy indignation, prayed that it might not rain in Israel - and for more than three years, not a drop of rain fell. Streams dried up, crops failed, and people starved.

Later, all alone, the prophet stood on Mt. Carmel among 450 prophets of Baal, proving the impotence of their false god.

In a spectacular demonstration of the power of the one true God, Elijah called fire down from heaven - and then directed the execution of Baal's priests.

Imagine the courage it took for one solitary man to pray for judgment on his own people, confront a wicked king, then stand before hundreds of false prophets and challenge their piety! Although the Lord took Elijah to heaven long ago, this courageous prophet still proclaims today that true leadership may mean standing alone and speaking difficult truth.[12]

Characteristics of Leviathan:

a. Never hears right.
b. Scrambles what a speaker is really trying to say.
c. Does not hear in a way a speaker intended.

d. Proud.
e. Won't say "I am sorry" and mean it or "Please forgive me" from the heart.
f. Creates jealousy, selfish ambition.
g. Quarrelsome.
h. Causes strife in homes, ministries, businesses, etc.
i. Leviathan retards spiritual growth and development and impairment of the senses of one's spirit.

PRAY AGAINST BIG THREE:

BAAL:

- Dear Lord Jesus,
- I confess and repent of every place I, or my ancestors, have walked in agreement with Baal.
- I repent and turn from his wicked ways.
- I want to follow you Jesus!
- I ask you to grant me a divorce from the principality of Baal, the ruler of demons.
- I want nothing to do with this evil principality.
- Lord Jesus, I want You and You alone.
- I decree: I am divorced from Baal and married to the Lord Jesus Christ now and always. Amen!"
- Father, in Jesus' Name, I ask you destroy Baal's stronghold, bind his strongmen, and cast his demons far from me and my country. (Expel!)

Queen of Heaven:

- Father, I confess and repent of every place I, or my ancestors, have walked in agreement with the Queen of Heaven.
- I repent and turn from her wicked ways.
- I renounce the Queen of Heaven, the political spirit and the corporate spirits of religion.
- Holy Spirit, I confess where I and my ancestors have grieved, resisted, or quenched you.
- Holy Spirit, I choose to keep in step with you.

✝ I hereby now proclaim:

✝ I believe in God the Father, - the God of Abraham, Isaac and Israel. I believe that only He is worthy of any worship, honor, reverence and glory.

✝ I believe in God the Son, Jesus as the one and only Mediator between the Father and man, and that the Holy Spirit acts only in this name. I believe that we need no other or additional mediator. I believe that man gets saved only in this name, by grace through faith. I believe that the Father bestows every good thing on man and mankind in this name.

✝ I believe in God the Holy Spirit and trust Him to seal me, fill me, baptize me, and lead me.

✝ Thus, I pray that the mighty and powerful hand of Almighty Father will keep me pure and steadfast on this road. In the Name of his Son I now proclaim that the Queen of Heaven has no power over me, and that the blood of Jesus is against her.

✝ Father, in Jesus' Name, I ask you destroy Queen of Heaven's stronghold, bind her strongmen, and cast her demons far from me and my church. (Expel!)

Leviathan:

✝ Heavenly Father, I confess and repent of any place where I or my ancestors, have walked in agreement with the Leviathan.

✝ "Lord, I ask you to remove from my life any influence from the spirit of Leviathan.

✝ I reject this spirit completely and whole-heartedly.

✝ Forgive me for any ways that I have served this spirit either intentionally or inadvertently.

✝ Forgive me for any ways in which I have been twisted or have twisted the truth, that I have listened to distortion of the truth or have distorted the truth.

✝ I devote myself to bringing unity, not division, into the church and will therefore honour other members and those you have placed in authority.

✝ By your grace I will speak the truth in love and dedicate myself to expressing the truth of your word in my life, in the precious name of Jesus. Amen."[14]

✝ Father, in Jesus' Name, I ask you destroy Leviathan's stronghold, bind his strongmen, and cast his demons far from me and my ministry. (Expel!)

Endnotes:

[1] Word Origin and History for leviathan.
http://click.reference.com/click/nn1ov4?clkpage=dic&clksite=dict&clkld=0&clkdest=http%3A%2F%2Fdictionary.reference.com%2Fcite.html%3Fqh%3Dleviathan%26ia%3Detymon2&clkmseg=15
[2]http://www.ancient.eu/user/jvdc/
[3]https://www.biblegateway.com/resources/hitchcocks-bible-names-dictionary/Heading-A
[4]https://www.biblegateway.com/resources/eastons-bible-dictionary/Heading-A
[5]https://www.biblegateway.com/resources/smiths-bible-names-dictionary/toc
[6]I originally found this picture at the following website, but this address no longer calls this picture up.
http://www.illuminatithe.com/world%20order.html
[7]http://www.atam.org/Phallicworship.html
[8]http://www.theforbiddenknowledge.com/hardtruth/symbolism_index.htm[8]
[9]http://beginningandend.com/beyonce-channels-the-spirit-of-jezebel-in-illuminati-ghosthaunted-video/ (Note: I do not recommend this article, especially for immature or young believers)
[10]Picture from article on the other names of Isis
https://thequeenofheaven.files.wordpress.com/2010/08/c384gyptischer_maler_um_1360_v-_chr-_001.jpg
[11]http://www.rightwingwatch.org/content/rick-perry-partners-apostle-who-thinks-statue-liberty-demonic-idol#sthash.aRDpOil2.dpuf
[12]John Maxwell's Leadership Promises - Be Willing to Stand Be Willing to Stand Up on October 5, 2015. You can sign up for his free daily devotionals at: http://iequip.us8.list-manage.com/track/click?u=2a567e582b37f53704fecc99b&id=301c0389ea&e=e19b211d47

[13]"Prayer researched and compiled by Eben Swart of Trumpet Call, Cape Town, South Africa.
www.trumpetcall.co.za."http://trumpetcall.co.za/prayers/the-queen-of-heaven.
[14]Defeating the Leviathan Spirit, Colin Urquhart. 4/28/2001.
http://www.colinurquhart.com/Article/19/Defeating-the-Leviathan-Spirit.aspx

Please note: I tried and retried each of these web addresses with success, but some of them did not work when I rechecked them on my final revision.

ABOUT THE AUTHOR

Douglas Carr never attended a church service until he went to liturgical church vacation bible school in sixth or seventh grade. At first he was intrigued by the greatness of God, but soon his experience turned from any hope of a bonified relationship with God apart from religious activity.

Doug gave little thought to God until after he married very young and discovered life was bigger than he was. A friend from work witnessed to him and Doug went on a spiritual quest for the span of six months. He even prayed the "sinner's prayer" every night until he became so frustrated he shouted to God "Can't I even trust you to save me?"

He became very involved in an evangelical church and people thought he had become a Christian, but all Doug experienced was personal reformation through self-effort and determination. He wasn't transformed by the power of God until salvation was clearly explained at a Basic Youth Conflicts Seminar taught by Bill Gothard. Finally, Doug came to know Jesus as Savior and Lord.

Within a year Doug sensed the call to ministry and wanted to work with Youth for Christ (YFC). To be employed by YFC, he was required to go to college, so while rearing a young family, and working full time with YFC, he attended Spring Arbor College where he earned a Bachelor's Degree in four years.

Doug took his first church during summer break between his junior and senior years of college. He was transferred to another church in a couple of years and continued pastoring for a total of twelve years. By that time he had become so proud that God mercifully and greatly humbled him. Through his own pride, sin, and ignorance he became a single father of three precious children, resigned his church, and tried to find peace and meaning in what many consider secular work.

Being a preacher and teacher is not something a called person does – it is who he or she is. Doug was successful outside of professional ministry but he was miserable. God was busy, however, at bringing Doug into a place of grace and relationship with Him that would allow him to break through strongholds of religion and pride and into victory in and through friendship with Jesus Christ.

After five years in the crucible of God's refining fire, Doug was offered a church near where he lived in Sturgis Michigan. He thought he would settle down into doing ministry as he had before—but God had other plans.

After six and a half years of singleness, God mercifully allowed Doug to marry a budding prophet, Pamela. At the time Doug didn't believe in extra-biblical revelation. His desire to hear God directly increased when he asked for Pam's hand in marriage and her reply was, "Let me ask God, and I will tell you what He says." Wow! Doug prayed hard that Pam would hear God's voice saying, "Yes, go with the man."

Thankfully, God told her to marry Doug and so began an incredible journey of getting to know God in whole new ways together in life and ministry.

Through a series of events, including: a forty-day fast, being introduced to new wineskins of life and ministry through Wagner Leadership Institute, introduction to Breakthrough Apostolic Ministries Network and Barbara Yoder, acceptance into membership of the International Society of Deliverance Ministries, and the chance to minister deep healing and deliverance to hundreds who were searching for answers seldom found in typical churches, Doug's calling went through metamorphosis into what it is today.

Doug began developing Free Indeed Seminars which are designed to lead individuals into personal freedom in such a way they will be able to minister the same to others. Soon he was lead to write books to help others grow in understanding and effectiveness in deliverance and inner healing ministry.

Doug and Pam, through a series of prophetic words and events, were moved to drastically down-size their home and schedules to make themselves more available to learn, minister, and advance the Kingdom of God.

Doug believes Jesus is cleansing His bride, preparing for the marriage feast of the Lamb. Together with Holy Spirit, Doug and Pam are being used in worship, teaching, writing, and Kingdom ministry. They walk in humble amazement that God has chosen to use them. To God be the Glory – Thine is the Kingdom, the Power, and the Glory, forever and ever, amen.

Endorsements

Busting Through to Greater Freedom will be a great help for people working through the sticky stuff of deliverance where problems continue even after foundational issues have been addressed. This work is beneficial for those working out their own salvation with fear and trembling, as well as for professional deliverance ministers who are often called to minister to more difficult cases which need help beyond basic deliverance and deep inner healing.

Bill Sudduth
President, Righteous Acts Ministries, Inc.
Apostolic Leader, International Society of Deliverance Ministers
Email: office@ramministry.org
Website: www.ramministry.org

Freedom is a gift to be cherished and guarded. True freedom is a rare commodity even in the Christian Community. God has gifted Apostle Doug Carr to spell out the steps to freedom. He writes out of what he has learned and become. Let this book go deep in your heart and guard it with all that you are!

Barbara J Yoder
Lead Apostle, Shekinah
Regional Apostolic Center
www.shekinahchurch.org
www.barbarayoderblog.com

Made in the USA
Middletown, DE
03 September 2024

60227382R00095